Seeing Lhasa

SEEING LHASA

British Depictions of the Tibetan Capital 1936–1947

Edited by
Clare Harris
&
Tsering Shakya

SERINDIA PUBLICATIONS
Chicago

A Group of Nine Tibetan Men in a Tent
(opposite title page)
Hugh Richardson, *c.* 1936–1950

The identities of the sitters in this group are not known. Richardson may have taken the picture at a Lhasa party – which were often held in tents.
PRM 2001.59.18.11.1.

This publication is issued in conjunction with the exhibition *Seeing Lhasa: British Depictions of the Tibetan Capital 1936–1947* organized by the Pitt Rivers Museum, Oxford, UK (7 September 2003–November 2004) and the Tenth Seminar of The International Association for Tibetan Studies (Oxford, 6–12th September 2003).

Published in 2003 by
Serindia Publications, Inc.
PO Box 10335
Chicago, IL 60610
www.serindia.com

ISBN 1-932476-04-0

Library of Congress Cataloguing-In-Publication Data
A CIP record of this book is available from the Library of Congress.

Designed and Typeset by Toby Matthews, Oxford, UK
Copy-editing by Donald Dinwiddie
Printed and bound in China

Contents

Preface

The Pitt Rivers Museum is one of the world's great museums of anthropology and archaeology in terms of the size, range and historical importance of its collections. Housed in a Victorian building in central Oxford, it embraces material from all corners of the world and all periods of human history, with approximately 275,000 artefacts, 125,000 historical photographs and 60 collections of manuscripts.

This book, and the exhibition to which it refers, were inspired by recent donations of photographs, albums and film made by British visitors to Tibet: Harry Staunton, Evan Nepean and Hugh Richardson. These fascinating collections complement other photographs from Tibet held at the museum (such as those made by Charles Bell, Henry Martin and Frederick Spencer Chapman) but as they all relate to the years between 1936 and 1947 we were presented with an opportunity to focus on a key period in Anglo-Tibetan relations. At this time, the visual documentation of Tibet assumed a high priority in the diplomatic agenda of scholar-officials such as Basil Gould and Hugh Richardson. It now presents us with perhaps the most concentrated and complex visual account of Tibet prior to the drastic events of the 1950s and thereafter. In an attempt to move beyond the exotic stereotypes that images of Tibet have often fostered, we have contextualised this material with essays, captions and biographical notes. It is hoped that this book will provide stimulation to both Tibetans and non-Tibetans to see Lhasa as it was but also in a fresh light.

'Seeing Lhasa' also includes the work of two artists – the Indian painter, Kanwal Krishna (some of whose Lhasa paintings are exhibited for the first time in the exhibition and illustrated in this book) and the Leverhulme Artist in Residence at the Pitt Rivers Museum (2003), Gonkar Gyatso, a contemporary artist who was born in Lhasa. The exhibition was devised, researched and designed by Clare Harris (Curator of Asian Collections). Elizabeth Edwards (Head of Photographic and Manuscript Collections at the museum) and Tsering Shakya acted as consultants to the project. Our thanks to Anthony Aris for his help and advice throughout.

Michael O'Hanlon, Director, Pitt Rivers Museum, Oxford

Acknowledgements

The Pitt Rivers Museum (University of Oxford), Serindia Publications (Chicago) and the authors would like to thank:

Anthony and Marie Laure Aris, Josh Bell, Khaushik Bhaumik, T. Richard Blurton, John Brooks at Isis Creative Framing, Krystyna Cech, Country and Eastern Ltd, Roger Croston, Tsering Dhundup, Donald Dinwiddie, John Eskenazi, Claire Freeman, Rupert Gill, Judy Goldthorp, Dick and Erica Gould, Gill Grant, Philip Grover, Gonkar Gyatso, Susan Aylmer Hall, Gerard Hanson, Diana Hughes, Ashish Krishna, The Leverhulme Trust, Donald Lopez, Toby Matthews, Hansjörg Mayer, The late Sir Evan Nepean and his widow Lady Cicely Nepean, Olivia Nepean, Bill Pagan and the Executors of the Richardson Estate, Anna Maria Rossi, Fabio Rossi, Gustav Roth, Kate Saunders, Chitrangada Sharma, Tadeusz Skorupski and Gill Stevens.

Special thanks are due to Malcolm Osman, Pitt Rivers Museum photographer, for his work on the scans used in this publication and the exhibition. We are also indebted to students taking the Oxford MSc. in Visual Anthropology (Nicole Barnabee, John Hayton and Jessica White) for preparing the DVD loop of archival film footage and to Eleanor Cooper, Katrina Crear, Martha Hildebrand, Lisa Maddigan and Helena Winston (MSc. in Material Anthropology and Museum Ethnography) for the guide to Tibetan objects on display in the Pitt Rivers Museum. Rhianedd Smith (M.Phil) and Fuyubi Nakamura (D.Phil) provided invaluable assistance with research and other preparations for the exhibition and book.

Note on the Use of Tibetan Terms

As Tibetan orthography can appear confusing for the general reader we have used a phonetic form adapted from Richardson (1998) throughout this book and provided Tibetan transliteration for key terms and names in the index.

For our sons, Riga Shakya and Luke Gill
in the hope that they will see Lhasa many times.

Seeing Lhasa: British Photographic and Filmic Engagement with Tibet 1936–1947

Clare Harris

In what is probably the most famous fictionalised account of British colonialism, Rudyard Kipling's eponymous hero Kim begins his journey of self-discovery in the company of a Tibetan monk. The Teshoo Lama (has left his monastery in Tibet some 'four months march' away) and entered British India on foot determined to visit the sacred sites of Buddhism.[1] His pilgrimage begins in the Lahore Museum or 'Wonder House' as 'the natives call' it, a setting which allows Kipling to introduce one of the key issues underlying his narrative: the tension between the purported certainties of Western scientific and academic knowledge versus the mysteries of Asian religions. In this dichotomous relationship, the museum stands as a metonym for the production of colonial knowledge where empiricism and positivism are the governing principles, for as Kim tells the Lama: 'That is the Government's house and there is no idolatry in it, but only a Sahib with a white beard'.[2] The Sahib-Curator of the museum (clearly modelled on Kipling's father, Lockwood, who served as curator of the Lahore Museum from 1874–1894) is the personification of the colonial enterprise in its benign scholarly form. He is custodian of a horde of Asian religious objects whose presence justifies the curator's credo: 'Here be the images, and I am here ... to gather knowledge.'[3] When presented with these 'images', which include Gandharan sculptures of buddhas and bodhisattvas and representations of the sacred sites he hopes to visit, the Tibetan is suitably awestruck by the contents of the museum. His sense of wonder is not, however, stimulated by idolatry, but rather by amazement at the extent of the Empire's accumulated knowledge.

The Potala Palace from the East (opposite)
Frederick Spencer Chapman, 1936–1937

The Potala Palace showing the watch tower on its eastern side. A group of Tibetans (including monks) can be seen walking away from Lhasa. They may have completed the route of the Lingkhor (sacred walk) around the city in order to gain merit and the chance of a better rebirth. Lhasa was a site of pilgrimage for people from all over Tibet. Due to its height, the Potala dominates the landscape of the Lhasa valley, serving as a visual as well as a spiritual focus for the city. Western visitors were often overwhelmed by this awe-inspiring sight.
PRM 1998.131.297.

Then, in a masterstroke of curatorial authority, the Sahib shows the lama a large album in which 'perched on its crag, overlooking the gigantic valley of many hued strata' is a photograph of the very monastery he has left behind in Tibet. The monk exclaims in incredulity 'Ay, Ay! ... And thou – the English, know of these things?'[4] At this moment, the Tibetan is initiated into the miraculous powers of Western science and the technologies of Empire, whose purview is demonstrated to extend far beyond the confines of British India and into Tibet. The imperial techniques for knowing and controlling subject nations – including the accurate mensuration of mapping and census-taking have been augmented by other scholarly pursuits which allow the curator to regale the monk with accounts of the successes of Orientalism. Not only have the locations associated with the life of the Buddha been unearthed by archaeologists and the texts of Buddhism analysed by linguists, but the very secrets of Tibetan religion and topology have been photographed and recorded for the colonial archive. This is the 'civilising mission' of the British Empire so famously summarised in 1900 by the Viceroy of India, Lord Curzon: 'It is equally our duty to dig and discover, to classify, reproduce and describe, to copy and decipher, and to cherish and conserve.'[5]

The Tibetan Foreign Affairs Ministry
Hugh Richardson, *c.* 1942?

The Tibetan Ministry of Foreign Affairs was founded in 1942. This photograph records the members of the ministry, including the two Foreign Secretaries (seated): Liushar (reperesenting monastic interests) and Surkhang Dzasa (representing lay interests). In a letter announcing the terms of reference for the bureau, it was noted that, 'In future, all matters both big and small, between the British and Tibetan Governments should be discussed with this office.' (See Goldstein 1989:381) Note that Surkhang is wearing glasses.
PRM 2001.59.18.18.1.

Sir Basil Gould and Tibetan Officials at the Potala
Harry Staunton, February 1940

Sir Basil Gould and a group of Tibetan officials climbing the steps leading into the Potala Palace. This photograph may well have been taken on the day when the British party was invited to attend part of the Installation of the 14th Dalai Lama. Gould (in bowler hat) is shown with a camera. Before he left London for Tibet Gould purchased a ciné camera and selected one which would suit 'a man who knew nothing at all about ciné photography'. (1957:200) He saw this as a good way of keeping in touch with his children back home in England. The camera was also used to record the Installation ceremony.
PRM 1999.23.1.15.3.

The moment of revelation in the 'Wonder House' is consummated by an exchange of gifts wherein the monk receives a pair of English unscratchable 'crystal' spectacles and the Sahib gains an old Chinese style pencase to which 'the collector's heart in the Curator's bosom had gone out to from the start'.[6] With this transaction, a message of benevolent colonialism is articulated in which the curator can preserve the artefactual remains of Tibetan culture whilst the Tibetan's vision is magically cleansed of centuries of distortion. Both the viewing of the photographic image of his monastery and the acquisition of the crystal glasses bring the Tibetan monk into the world of Western systems of viewing – of seeing through focused lenses and being seen by others through the eminently portable vehicle of photography.[7] As we shall see, Kipling's nineteenth century dramatisation of this entanglement between East and West has the flavour of premonition about it, for in the first half of the twentieth century Anglo-Tibetan relations become increasingly marked by both a literal and representational exchange of views. The fictional meeting in the 'Wonder House' at Lahore was re-enacted in 1940 when the British political officer Sir Basil Gould attended the Installation ceremonies of the 14th Dalai Lama in Lhasa. Amongst his gifts to the newly recognised Tibetan leader was a pair of field glasses.[8] In exchange Gould received the unique opportunity of being the first European to witness the installation of a Dalai Lama and to photograph it.[9]

This essay and the exhibition to which it refers are attempts to bring the issue of vision (and the visual cultures in which it operates)

to greater prominence in our understanding of Tibet. In examining the photographic and filmic materials made by the British in Lhasa between 1936, the date of Sir Basil Gould's Mission to Lhasa, and 1947, the year when India gained its independence from Britain, we do not seek to produce a kind of visual ethnography of the Tibetan capital nor to celebrate the British view of the city so highly desirable to colonial cadres in the early twentieth century.[10] Rather, we begin by taking a step back from both the archive and the content of images in order to analyse their production and use in the context of the period in which they were created. Recent research has given great emphasis to the ways in which Tibet has been imagined by non-Tibetans,[11] but much of this scholarship has concentrated on textual forms of recording rather than the visual products of encounters between Tibetans and the foreigners who visited them. Yet the need for a visual trigger to ideas about the country was evident at least as far back as the eighteenth century as, for example, when the Italian Augustinian monk Antonius Georgius included line drawings alongside the text for his encyclopedic *Alphabetum Tibetananum* (1763). Some of the subjects he selected for visual depiction – prayer wheels, stupas and the apparatus of religious processions have since been repeatedly selected by photographers, artists and publishers as representative samples of Tibetan material culture. The technologies of mass production have enabled such images to be repeated to the point of cliché, but the status of such visual information in epistemological terms remains illustrative and descriptive.

It seems that photography and other kinds of imagery concerning Tibet (including painting and film) have been deemed unworthy of the close reading and context-driven historical analysis which are so essential to the task of literary scholarship.[12] In this vein, we might continue by noting that just as the text is acknowledged in most quarters to be the product of a relationship between reader and writer (and many other factors beyond these), so in contemporary thinking about material/visual culture the object is acknowledged to be the nexus of a set of relationships between actors operating according to a range of personal and collective cultural codes.[13] Importantly such objects are also thought to have a 'life' beyond the moment of inception,[14] which sees them moving within networks of exchange (for example) and through different contextualising moments or interpretative frameworks. Photographs, perhaps pre-eminently, exhibit this concept, in that the life of a photograph can extend far beyond the setting in and for which it was first made as it circulates amongst new communities of viewers and extends its

The 14th Dalai Lama (Opposite)
Unknown Chinese photographer, 1939

Portrait of Tenzin Gyatso at the time of his identification as the 14th Dalai Lama in Amdo. Spencer Chapman Collection.
PRM 1998.131.630.

Monks on the 'Golden Procession'
Hugh Richardson, *c.* 1936–1950

The 'Golden Procession' at the foot of the Potala Palace. This image records the start of events on the 30th day of the second month of the ceremonial year when a set of sacred objects including texts and thangka *paintings are paraded around the Potala Palace. The* Ser treng *or 'Golden Procession of the Assembly of Worship' was instituted by the Regent Sangye Gyatso (1653–1705) in commemoration of a vision seen by the 5th Dalai Lama(1617–1682). As the monks make their way around the Potala Palace, they are thought to create a golden rosary around the building.*
PRM 2001.59.9.33.1.

valency over time.[15] The most extreme form of this circulation is experienced by the contemporary global community of computer users who can conjure a picture of the Potala made decades ago in Lhasa at the touch of a button. However, though this technology is liberating in many ways (allowing for a democratising access to visual materials), it also threatens to return us to the days of Kipling and the numerous others who fashioned colonial records of non-Western peoples in a fictionalising or anonymising way. That is, as in nineteenth century Orientalist accounts of Tibet where even the most scholarly authors reduce their subjects to ethnographic 'types', we may be in danger of returning to a 'timeless' and 'nameless' sense of what and who is Tibetan.[16]

Examining, as we do here, images of Tibet produced at a very particular moment in time and emerging from particular encounters, is important. Not only are photographs of intrinsic value as visual documents, but they also present us with evidence of the development of present day 'Shangri-Laist' imagery of Tibet. They allow us to historicize the evolution of key Western tropes (such as particular ways of viewing the Potala Palace) and the invention of visual traditions associated with places such as Lhasa (including the repeated photo-documentation of ceremonies such as the Palden Lhamo procession and monastic masked dances – or *cham* – described by many British commentators as 'Devil Dances'). The density of the photographic record for certain subjects leads us to think that British photography of Tibet was interlinked over the course of the early twentieth century with colonial officers literally standing in the footsteps of their forebears to record the same photographic subject. Ultimately, we might argue that the close-reading of this photographic lineage allows us to critique the process by which we have (unwittingly) absorbed the influence of a colonial gaze and have learnt to 'see' Lhasa through the framing devices adopted by a powerful British elite. Their photographic engagement with Tibet (during a period of intense diplomatic activity in the 1930s and 1940s) stimulated the British public's imagination and created a demand for more of the same.

Hence the circulation of Tibetan photographs began well before the computer-era, as can be witnessed in a survey of books, magazines, lantern slide shows and albums produced from the 1880s onwards. In order to feed the clamour for Tibet-related imagery in such public and private contexts, the ascribed 'meanings' of photography were often altered, delimited or drastically curtailed through the addition of captions creating 'preferred' readings. To give just one example, we

Tsarong at the Steps of his Lhasa House
Frederick Spencer Chapman, 1936–1937

Dasang Damdul Tsarong was a favourite of the 13th Dalai Lama (1876–1933), a military man and later a Shapé of the Tibetan Cabinet (Kashag) until he was removed from office as a result of his modernising policies. He was a great friend of the 1936 British Mission, frequently inviting them to his house and accompanying them on their various visits around Lhasa. He was considered by the mission to be a great character, as Gould recalled: 'Once, after a long and festive party at the De Kyi Lingka, he fell asleep in my arms murmuring, "Great minister, I love you, I love you". At breakfast next morning he had his usual bright eye and was quite unperturbed. He spoke a little English. To him it seemed strange that anybody in India should not welcome British rule.' (1957:236) He had four wives (including Rigzin Choden, Pema Dolkar, Rinchen Dolma [later Mary Taring] and Tseten Dolkar) and ten children. Although he was in India in 1956, he insisted on going back to Tibet to help the 14th Dalai Lama to escape into exile. He was captured by the Chinese and in 1959 died mysteriously the night before what was due to be his public humiliation.
PRM 1998.131.477.

might turn to a photograph which appeared in the 1937 edition of the British film journal *Sight and Sound* accompanying an essay by Frederick Spencer Chapman entitled 'Tibetan Horizon'. In it, Spencer Chapman describes the ciné film he made during Sir Basil Gould's 1936 Mission to Lhasa (see below) and illustrates his points with his own still photography. Alongside a rear view of a 'nomad woman' (wearing an elaborate headdress), Spencer Chapman includes a portrait of a Tibetan man described as 'An official in ceremonial dress' (see left). This is, in fact, Dasang Damdul Tsarong, a member of the Tibetan government and perhaps the prime interlocutor between the British and the Tibetans in the 1930s. (A more detailed discussion of Tsarong's role is given below.) Though Spencer Chapman knew him well as the jovial aristocratic host of many a fine party in Lhasa, Tsarong has been 'ethnologised' according to the agenda of image consumption in popular journals. Instead of appearing as an historically significant individual, he has been forced to play the role of a representative Tibetan type.[17] By returning to the originating contexts for such images we can reinsert the specificity of their meanings. A socio-historical approach illuminates the narrative behind the relationships which make photography possible – such as the friendship between Tsarong and a British photographer-official like Spencer Chapman. These micro-histories enable us to invert the process of anonymisation and generalisation which has so often been the effect of early anthropological photography.

Looking at British imagery made in the period before the Chinese take-over, we can critique the production of certain myths and propagandistic renderings of the concept of Tibet. Amongst these, one of the most pernicious has defined Tibet as a 'forbidden land' – a country whose geographic location and religious culture made it inaccessible to outsiders. Though the Tibetans had undoubtedly pursued an isolationist policy in relation to Western visitors until the early twentieth century, Lhasa was in reality a relatively cosmopolitan place. For centuries it had been a centre of mercantile activity and by the 1930s traders and diplomats from other parts of Asia were in semi-permanent residence (such as Ladakhis, Nepalese and Chinese) and the Tibetans had been visited by an intrepid few from all corners of the globe – Germans, French, Italians, Scandinavians, Americans, Russians, Japanese and various parties of the British, some of whom came more than once. All recognised the importance of seeing Lhasa in a touristic and pioneering sense, but the British particularly focused on seeing and being seen by some of the most influential Tibetan figures in their seats of power. Coupled with this

Dasang Damdul Tsarong in New Year Dress (previous page)
Frederick Spencer Chapman, 1937

Dasang Damdul Tsarong wearing the dress of a high official at the New Year ceremony in 1937. Tsarong's chuba *(gown) is made from silk brocade with Chinese-style dragon motifs. His gold, turquoise and coral '*sog gil*' (ear-ring) indicates his status as a high-ranking layman in the Tibetan government. A strict dress code applied at ceremonial occasions such as this and Tibetans were told what to wear depending on their rank. As Spencer Chapman recalls: 'I had the impression of watching some gay medieval pageant, some fantastic Hollywood production, or a throng of people in fancy dress... Tsarong wore a glistening brocade dress with a multi-coloured pattern of scaly dragons'. (1938:120)*
PRM 1998.157.95.

diplomatic imperative, the visual record was seen as crucial and hence thousands of British photographs of the capital and its inhabitants now exist. But these images do not simply evoke a place of ethnographic curiosity nor replicate a severe separation between coloniser and colonised subject. The tone is one of intermingling – in social, aesthetic and technological registers. As we shall see, rather than a remote monoculture, Lhasa was a place of meetings and mirroring between elite members of the British colonial establishment and equally highly placed Tibetan aristocrats and religious leaders. Both parties saw aspects of themselves reflected in the 'other' they encountered. By the 1930s, they also shared a fascination with what was rapidly becoming one of the most powerful technologies of the twentieth century – the camera. This is a concept (and an experience) neatly summarised by Charles Hallisey in the term 'intercultural mimesis'. Hallisey exhorts us to acknowledge that, when representing any given culture, said culture will undoubtedly influence 'the investigator to represent (it) in a certain way.'[18] Beyond this, however, we must recognise those individuals (and collectivities) who participate in the production of representations and are, more than mere 'informants', actively present in the depiction of themselves.[19] Their contribution ensures that relations between (aspiring) coloniser and colonised are often reciprocal and mutually constitutive. These relationships suggest a refiguring of the classical sense of the term mimesis (found in Ovid) and the pool in which Narcissus contemplated himself. Rather than just thinking of a single reflective surface that records reality in an indexical way (an argument that is frequently cited

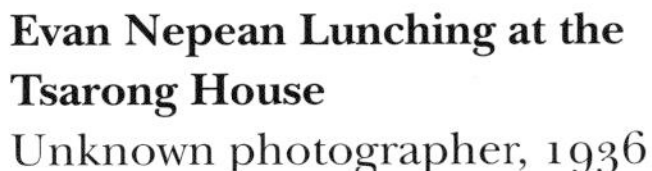

Evan Nepean Lunching at the Tsarong House
Unknown photographer, 1936

Dasang Damdul Tsarong, two of his wives and Evan Nepean eating lunch in the Tsarong house.
PRM 2001.35.386.

Abbots of Sera Monastery
Frederick Spencer Chapman, 1936–1937

Founded in 1419, the Geluk monastery of Sera was located just north of Lhasa. At the time of the 1936 Mission, it was the second largest monastery in the world, housing 5,500 monks. The abbots pictured here were in charge of the four colleges which made up the monastery.
PRM 1998.131.360.

The Palace of Reting Rinpoche, the Regent of Tibet
Frederick Spencer Chapman, 1936–1937

The Regent's palace was newly built at the time of the 1936 Mission, and lay on the outskirts of Lhasa near Sera monastery. 'The palace is very small, containing only storerooms on the ground floor and a single sitting-room above; but it is an attractive building and beautifully decorated. There are golden turrets on the roof, and along the top of the wall the usual golden emblems on a matt background of willow-twig walling. The woodwork around the windows is cleverly carved and painted in bright colours. Boxes of gay flowers stand on every window-sill protected from the sun by awnings of white cloth. Moreover, the palace lies in a walled garden with well-kept lawns, and beds full of English flowers in luxurious bloom.' Spencer Chapman (1938: 99–100)
PRM 1998.157.36.

The Regent, Reting Rinpoche (opposite)
Hugh Richardson, *c.* 1936–1947

Reting Rinpoche (Thupten Jamphel Yeshe Gyaltsen), the Regent of Tibet, sitting in the garden of his house with two dogs. The spaniels are probably those presented to him by the 1936 British Mission as a gift from the Viceroy of India. Spencer Chapman (1938) notes that the Regent was a great lover of animals (and already owned a number of dogs) but that when presented with the spaniels he could barely conceal his delight. The Regent appeared far more relaxed with the members of the Mission when they visited him in his own home (to show films and play music) than on official, public occasions.
PRM 2001.59.18.14.1.

Wangchen Gelek Surkhang
Frederick Spencer Chapman,
1936–1937

Surkhang Se in gyaluche *dress at New Year. Wangchen Gelek Surkhang came from one of the older of Tibet's aristocratic families. The Surkhangs were said to be descended from the 4th Dalai Lama (1589–1617) whose grandfather had been the chief of the Qoshot Mongols who gave the Dalai Lamas their title. In 1936, Surkhang was a junior official in the Tibetan government (having a small job under Tsarong in the Tibetan Mint), but by 1943 he had become a Kalon at the very young age of thirty-three. He had attended the school set up by Frank Ludlow in Lhasa for a year, and had learnt some English there. His father was also a government minister and acted as one of the heads of the Foreign Affairs Bureau.*
PRM 1998.131.494.

for the filmic traces of photography – that is, the photograph is an indexical record of the 'real world' because it is produced from the effects of light touching the chemical surface of film), perhaps we could consider photography through the concept of a two-way mirror whose fluid transparency enables both the producers and subjects of images to 'see' and construct a sense of one another. This is the underlying principle behind the exhibition 'Seeing Lhasa': to show how the British saw Tibet and Tibetans and to analyse the ways in which their depictions may be said to record an active return of the colonial gaze on the part of their subjects. For just as there is no such thing as the 'innocent eye',[20] so the photograph is never innocent of the cultural context in which it comes into being. In these encounters the camera creates rather than reveals the observable realities of Lhasa and the photographic object becomes the site of multiple agency.

Lhasa: The Dream Destination

Published in 1901, Kipling's novel undoubtedly capitalised on the current state of British knowledge about Tibet, particularly that which could be derived from popular books and museum collections. In the late nineteenth century, research on the country which lay beyond the Himalayas and the political boundaries of the British Empire was often an extension of Orientalist approaches to Indian religious and cultural practices. Tibetan Buddhism was to be investigated as a (probably) corrupted form of the purer Buddhism of the subcontinent. Due to the difficulties of entering Tibet, the 'fieldwork' for this scholarship was often conducted in the Tibetanised areas of British India such as Ladakh, Kalimpong and Darjeeling or in Sikkim, an independent state under British 'protection.' A key text of this period *The Buddhism of Tibet or Lamaism* (1894) was produced in this way by a Government of India employee, L. A. Waddell. From 1885 to 1895, Waddell laboured on the periphery of Tibet under the unglamourous title of Assistant Sanitary Commissioner for Sikkim and Darjeeling, but this vocation provided him with ample opportunity to examine the inhabitants of the Himalayas, particularly Tibetans. His 570-page book virtually became the training manual for Raj employees who aspired to become Tibet specialists, and was circulated widely back home in Britain. However, *The Buddhism of Tibet* had to be illustrated with line drawings and a handful of photographs produced in the studio of Johnston and Hoffmann, the portrait photographers who had an outpost of their Calcutta-based business in Darjeeling, which was frequented by Tibetans and the British (on their vacations from the heat of the plains).[21] This problem could only be amended by acquiring photographs made in Tibet and so, like many others in his situation, Waddell dreamt of expanding his knowledge by visiting the country in person. With the Youngshusband Expedition of 1903–1904, his dreams were realised. Waddell was appointed as surgeon and 'Antiquarian to the Force', charged with collecting material for the British Museum. Alongside these duties, the first concerted British attempt to photograph Tibet began and a

The Regent's Tents in front of the Potala Palace
Frederick Spencer Chapman, 1936

Appliqué tents decorated with auspicious Buddhist motifs were popular in Central Tibet and were often used at religious festivals or for picnic parties in the summer. The procession for which these tents were erected was probably the return of the Regent from Reting on 23 November 1936. The Regent's luggage and tents were sent ahead of him to Lhasa, and in his honour a line of stones were placed on either side of the road with improvised incense burners built out of earth and painted white every hundred yards. The official reception took place a mile from Lhasa in a place called the 'Garden of the Mystics' and was attended by both the British and the Chinese representatives.
PRM 1998.131.531.

pattern of British action which combined diplomacy with photography was established.

The expedition led by Colonel Francis Younghusband was arguably the closest Britain came to mounting an invasion of Tibet. Younghusband set off to reach the Tibetan capital, Lhasa, with a large contingent of troops to assist his passage – despite the Tibetan government's conviction that foreigners should be repelled. He reached his destination and forced the Tibetans to sign the 1904 Anglo Tibetan convention, but only after a number of brutal battles along the way. The mission also failed to establish a permanent base in the Tibetan capital. However, the British public avidly consumed newspaper accounts of the Colonel's exploits which were wired back to London by the *Daily Mail* correspondent accompanying the mission, Edmund Candler. As Peter Bishop suggests (in his pioneering study of Tibetan travel literature, *The Myth of Shangri-La*), it was perhaps the very fact that Tibet was never fully colonised nor conquered that ignited such potent imaginings about it. I would also like to suggest here that it was the lack of images of Tibet that initially fired the public's enthusiasm for first-hand textual accounts of the 'land on the roof of the world'. Whilst Tibet remained inaccessible for photographic documentation, the text took up the 'burden of representation'[22] – in marked contrast to the situation in India during the mid- to late-nineteenth century when large-scale photographic projects like 'The People of India' created a kind of visual saturation of the South Asian subject. The desire for publications which would reveal Tibet's secrets is demonstrated by the titles of popular books such as *Lhasa: the Hidden City* or *Lhasa: the Mysterious*. Candler's book-length account of his visit was published as 'The Unveiling of Lhasa' in 1905, but this work was unillustrated and the true task of unveiling Lhasa to the gaze of the British public fell to Waddell, who also published an account of the mission in the same year. As Stanley Abe notes: 'Undoubtedly one of the most impressive aspects of Waddell's *Lhasa and its Mysteries* was its visual documentation of Tibet: three colour photographs, each identified as having been taken "from nature", 110 black-and-white photographs and numerous drawings, maps and charts.'[23] With this lavishly illustrated and scholarly volume, Waddell established a pattern which was to be emulated by many of his successors as British colonial officers in Tibet.[24]

Sir Charles Bell, the Maharajah of Sikkim and the 13th Dalai Lama
Johnston & Hoffman, 1910

This image with a painted background and Bell in uniform was taken in the studio of Johnston and Hoffman in Calcutta.
PRM 1998.285.431.

With fears that the Chinese or Russians would expand their influence in Tibet, the Government of India (i.e. the British colonial regime in India) spent the early decades of the twentieth century trying to establish more settled diplomatic and trade relations with their northerly neighbour. The highest-ranking post established to deal with these matters was that of Political Officer for Sikkim, Bhutan and Tibet and between 1904 and 1921 that position was frequently occupied by Sir Charles Bell. Bell must be mentioned here as he was perhaps the archetypal British officer: the son of a member of the Indian Civil Service, educated in the classic mould of colonial cadres at Winchester and Oxford (where he took 'Greats' or Classical Studies), and a career diplomat who became such a dedicated admirer of Tibetan culture that he published five books on the subject.[25] Bell also produced several hundred photographs of Tibet (assisted by the Sikkimese Rabden Lepcha) and was probably the first Englishman to have become truly close to a Tibetan dignitary, the 13th Dalai Lama.[26] Bell's approach to Tibet – which required that cadres should learn the Tibetan language and immerse themselves in the study of the place before attempting any diplomacy – was to set the agenda until Indian Independence in 1947, when British relations with Tibet were rapidly curtailed. In the meantime, Bell's followers repeatedly sought to set up a permanent British Mission in Lhasa.

A Side Street in the Centre of Lhasa
(overleaf)
Frederick Spencer Chapman, 1936

A side street in the Barkhor area of central Lhasa with Tibetans waiting to view the Palden Lhamo procession. In the foreground is a pile of mustard straw with a torma offering of butter and barley flour ready to be burnt. This photograph was taken on 28 November 1936, on the occasion of the annual procession of an effigy of the protectoress Palden Lhamo through the streets of Lhasa. Spencer Chapman took photographs from the roof of the Surkhang family house.
PRM 1998.131.576.

The ribald street songs of Lhasa give a flavour of the Tibetan response to British encroachment on their territory:

> *At first they were known as enemies of the faith;*
> *And then they were known as 'foreigners'.*
> *But when (we) saw their English dollars,*
> *We called them Honourable Shahib.* [27]

This song was recited after Younghusband entered Lhasa but it took a couple of decades for the British to realise that the Tibetan desire for the 'English dollar' could help to ease their path. Hence by the time Sir Basil Gould took up the post of Political Officer for Sikkim, Bhutan and Tibet in 1935, his policy was decidedly gentler than that of the Younghusband era and was designed to coax Tibetans into good relations with the British through a series of social and cultural devices which can be summarised as: food, film, finance and football. Gould's subtle diplomacy meant that he and his team managed to stay in Lhasa for more than six months. He also became one of the few foreigners invited to Lhasa by the Tibetan authorities to attend the installation of the 14th (current) Dalai Lama in 1940. Perhaps most importantly Gould was able to create the post of 'Head of the British

Members of the British Mission to Lhasa 1936–1937
Frederick Spencer Chapman, 1936–1937

From left to right (back row standing): Sidney Dagg, Frederick Spencer Chapman, Evan Nepean and Rai Bahadur Norbhu Dhondhup; (front row seated) Hugh Richardson, Sir Basil Gould, Dr. William Morgan. Dagg was a wireless operator, Spencer Chapman was the personal secretary to Gould, Nepean was another wireless operator, Norbhu was interpreter and diplomatic aide to the Mission, Richardson was British Trade Agent at Gyantse, Gould was Political Officer for Sikkim, Bhutan and Tibet, and in charge of this Mission to Lhasa, Morgan was the Mission doctor.
PRM 1998.131.378.

Nechung Monastery at the End of Year *Gutor* Ceremony
Frederick Spencer Chapman, 1937

The courtyard and entrance to the assembly chamber at Nechung monastery during the end of year ceremonies. On the 29th day of the twelfth lunar month the Tse Gutor *masked dance is performed at many Tibetan monasteries to purge the sins and misfortunes of the previous year in preparation for the new one. At the end of this ceremony the oracle of Nechung is possessed by the protector deity, Pehar, and gives his predictions for the coming year.*
PRM 1998.157.40.

***Tse Gutor* Masked Dance at the Potala Palace**
Frederick Spencer Chapman, 1937

The Tse Gutor *masked dance being performed by the monks of Namgye Tratsang in the eastern courtyard of the Potala. Richardson gives a detailed account of this event in* Ceremonies of the Lhasa Year*: 'The chief is the Chinese priest Hashang, a huge heavily padded figure in a scarlet robe and with a massive, smiling bald-headed mask. With him are two tiny child-like figures, two more in the dress of Indian sadhus, and two with death's head masks.' (1993:116–123) Then two more masked dancers arrive – one representing Shinje, the lord of the dead and protector of the Buddhist faith, and the other, the stag-headed Tsamuntri. Other dancers portray wrathful protector deities such as Dorje Jigje (with a bull's head), Tamdrin (the horse-headed), a red masked Mahakala and the black-faced Lhamo.*
PRM 1998.157.81.

Mission, Lhasa', a position which continued until 1947, and primarily occupied by his most illustrious successor, Hugh Richardson.[28]

Between 1936 and 1947, events of enormous significance were taking place around the world. Though Tibet was largely untouched by the horrors of the Second World War, the geo-political instability of the decade had implications for the land on the roof of the world. By 1947, India had gained its independence from the British Empire and (perhaps as a result) Tibet fell increasingly into the ambit of another colonising power: China. Hence the decade between Gould's first official mission to Lhasa and the end of British power in the subcontinent (to which this essay and exhibition refer) marks a turning point for the fortunes of both the British and Tibetan governments. By the end of the 1950s, thousands of Tibetans, including the Dalai Lama, fled from Lhasa never to set foot there again.

How might we describe the place from which so many Tibetans reluctantly departed? At an elevation of some 12,000 feet, Lhasa is the primary urban development in Ü, Tibet's central province. The history of the settlement of this site on the banks of the Kyi Chu river can be traced back to the Neolithic period. But for Tibetans the place is not only the domain of humans: the name, Lhasa, indicates that the city is also inhabited by gods (*lha*). Since the Yarlung dynasty (7th–9th centuries), it has also been home to some of Tibet's most revered religious, royal and secular leaders. From King Songtsen Gampo who built the first Buddhist temple in Tibet (the Jo khang) there in the mid-seventh century to the 5th Dalai Lama (1617–1682) who commissioned the massive edifice that is the Potala Palace a thousand years later, the built environment of Lhasa stands as a memorial to the power of Tibetan Buddhist institutions, secular governance and key individuals. The Dalai Lama's summer and winter palaces (the Norbulingka and the Potala) dominated the landscape whilst the Jo khang (sometimes dubbed the 'cathedral' of Lhasa, but should more correctly be termed the Tsuglakhang or 'central house'), was at the centre of the thriving Barkhor market area. Powerful religious institutions, such as the Gelukpa monasteries of Drepung and Sera, and the monastic base of the Nechung Oracle, who could divine the future of Tibet and much else, were on the outskirts of Lhasa. At the time of festivals and religious ceremonies, Lhasa became a Tibet in microcosm, as its population swelled with pilgrims from all over the country who sought a merit-accruing glimpse of these remarkable buildings. All these key sites were visited by the British between 1936 and 1947, and are still standing today, though many of the grand houses

Entrance to the Norbulingka
(opposite)
Frederick Spencer Chapman,
1936–1937

The entrance gateway to the Norbulingka ('The Jewel Park'), the Dalai Lama's summer palace in Lhasa. The Norbulingka consists of a large walled enclosure containing a number of buildings and fine gardens. Spencer Chapman described the entrance in some detail: 'The main gate is most impressive, with a roof of highly glazed tiles and the usual golden medallions on a background of dark red. On each side and above the gate is a system of branching woodwork painted red and picked out with flower-designs in bright colours. A row of grinning white demons look down from beneath the roof. The heavy wooden doors, with metal knockers formed by a ring held in the jaws of a lion, open into a portico, the ceiling of which is richly painted.' (1938:183)
PRM 1998.131.324.

Frederick Spencer Chapman
Evan Nepean, 1936

Frederick Spencer Chapman (1907–1971) standing by the Kyi Chu river with the Potala Palace in the background. This is one of the least formal shots taken during the 1936 British Mission to Lhasa. Taking a break from their duties, Spencer Chapman and Evan Nepean went swimming in the Kyi Chu. They then photographed one another on the river bank with their shirts off. Spencer Chapman often walked in the countryside around Lhasa bird-spotting, collecting botanical specimens and taking photographs. See biographical entry.
PRM 1998.131.399.

of the Tibetan aristocracy in which British visitors socialised have been torn down in the course of recent 'modernisation' campaigns. The British Mission house, the Dekyi Lingka, a building strategically selected to literally accommodate British interests within a local architectonic idiom, has also met the same fate.[29]

Despite this venerable history, the Lhasa visited by Sir Basil Gould and his team in the 1930s was beginning to modernise. Just as the country (Tibet) was not entirely isolated from international developments of a political or military nature, so its capital was by no means devoid of urban sophistication. When Gould arrived in Lhasa in 1936, there was electricity, a telegraphic machine and even a few cars, and he noted with pleasure that he could lie in bed within the shadow of the Potala listening to the chimes of Big Ben on his radio. By 1940, the Dalai Lama had his own telephone and many Tibetan aristocrats had radios. These were some of the physical indicators of a larger project designed to create a unified, modern Tibetan state in which Lhasa increasingly presented itself as a 'national' capital. As Alex McKay notes, these developments were in good measure influenced by the British, initially under the aegis of Gould's predecessor Charles Bell. 'In the decade between 1913 and 1923, following Bell's advice to the Dalai Lama, Tibet adopted most of the symbols and attributes of an independent state. It created its own flag, currency and stamps, determined its frontiers in agreement with the British, reorganised its economy, bureaucracy, and provincial government, and with British assistance, strengthened its military forces.'[30] Thus British involvement with these arrangements was clearly designed both to demarcate Tibet as a country independent of China (who had made claims for 'suzerainty' over their Western neighbour for centuries) and increasingly to bring it within the orbit of British India. Located in the southern central region of Tibet, on ancient trade routes which lead to Sikkim and thence to India, Lhasa was thus not merely a romantic dream destination, but the obvious target for British penetration into the heart of Tibetan society. In the 1930s and 1940s, the relationships established between elite members of the British colonial service and Lhasa's ruling class meant that both the historical and political image of Tibet became 'Lhasa-centric'.[31]

Lhasa in the Filmic Frame

> *The most phlegmatic person could hardly avoid a thrill, when marching up the Kyi chu, at the first sight of the Potala, the palace of the Dalai Lama with its gilded roofs glittering in the bright sunshine of these high altitudes, at many miles distance.*
>
> *Mission Diary*, 1936, 'August 24th, Monday, Lhasa 11,800 feet, 16 miles'

This excited note on the experience of seeing the Potala for the first time was recorded by Frederick Spencer Chapman – the official diarist of the Gould Mission to Tibet in 1936.[32] Like many a foreigner before and since, he waxes lyrical on the subject of

Harry Staunton with a Ciné Camera
Unknown photographer,
1940–1942

Harry Staunton was the British Mission doctor from 1940 to 1942, and, with Sir Basil Gould, one of only two Westerners to witness the Installation ceremony of the current (14th) Dalai Lama in Lhasa in 1940. Trained at St Bartholomew's Hospital London, he joined the Indian Medical Service in 1934, holding various posts around the country before being posted as Civil Surgeon to Bhutan and Tibet. He took black and white photographs while in Lhasa and made several reels of colour ciné film. See biographical entry.
PRM 1999.23.2.5.

the Dalai Lama's palace, which once glimpsed provides confirmation that Lhasa, the dream destination, will soon be reached. For contemporary Tibetans this sight inspires a rapid disembarkation from any vehicle they might be occupying to make prostrations at the roadside, even though they may be miles away from the object of their devotion. Spencer Chapman also experiences a kind of epiphany on the road to Lhasa, though his response is mediated through an awareness of Western accounts of this most 'striking building'. Beginning with the Jesuit Gruber in 1661, every visitor to the city thereafter made some reference to the Potala. A member of Younghusband's expedition commented on the enthusiasm with which his confrères competed to spot the Potala first. 'The hour teemed with fierce interest of a kind no man will perhaps ever feel again.... Here we thought there was to be seen a gleam of gold in the distance, and we thought that Lhasa was at last in sight.'[33] Bishop suggests that, by 1904, the Potala had become an emblem of the 'long process whereby Tibet was constructed as a sacred place in the Western imagination.'[34] But he also remarks on the sometimes conflicting ideas which the palace evoked. The golden majesty of its roofs contrasted sharply with the squalor and filth of Lhasa's backstreets, and for some this comparison disrupted expectations of otherworldliness and utopianism associated with Tibetan religion. However, members of the Gould Mission make little reference to the smoke and dirt of Lhasa (except where it interferes with the photographic process). For them, the acquisition of a golden view of Lhasa was a critical diplomatic and political matter whereas for us today, seeing the Potala through the British photographic record reveals something of the 'mechanisms of knowledge construction'[35] in operation at this time.

For those members of British missions to Lhasa equipped with a camera, 'Potala-spotting' was more than a hobby akin to birdwatching (though observing and recording flora and fauna was part of their colonial training), it was an activity which reflected a nascent touristic approach to Tibetan places. The Potala functioned as the backdrop for their increasing entanglement with ideas about Tibet which sometimes meant that the reality of their experiences burst the bubble of longing for exotica. Spencer Chapman and Evan Nepean, for example, photographed themselves standing shirtless in the Kyi Chu river with the Potala hovering in the distance.[36] Here the Tibetan landscape has been naturalised, as if its climate and topography were really not so different from those of Britain. The aesthetic of the British holiday snap – with its comic attitude to displays of flesh, is transposed to the Tibetan plateau. For many others, the Potala became something of an obsession, as the grand edifice that dominated the Lhasa skyline provoked repeated photographic engagements. Evan Nepean (the Gould Mission telegraph and radio operator) and Harry Staunton (the doctor who visited Lhasa with Gould in 1940), photographed it on several occasions and proudly displayed the results in their personal albums.[37] In this instance, the photograph performs the role of postcard, attesting that a visit to a site of special significance has been made and enabling friends and family of the Mission members to admire and empathise with the achievements of their relatives. Spencer Chapman and Hugh Richardson photographed the Potala at different times of day, in a variety of weather conditions and from every conceivable angle. Hugh Richardson's pictures are perhaps the most aestheticised and romantic, as if for him the Potala was an object of desire. Though critical by nature, Richardson 'lost his heart' to Tibet (as his boss Gould remarked),[38] and since the Potala was frequently thought to embody the nation, so Richardson's feelings seem to combine the admiration of Tibet with the form of the Potala. He lovingly frames her contours glimpsed from a distance through the gnarled trunks of willow trees, but at other moments stands reverentially at her feet to shoot her close up and from

The Potala Palace photographed through Willow Trees
Hugh Richardson, *c.* 1936–1950
PRM 2001.59.11.99.1.

a steep angle.[39] When dressed in the massive silk *thangka* displayed during New Year ceremonies (the Köku), the Potala is seen in her most imposing guise as the focus for events in the Tibetan Buddhist calendar which Richardson famously recorded in his book *Ceremonies of the Lhasa Year*. This account of religious ceremonial in Lhasa (covering all the major events in the course of a year) is the product of the exceptional circumstances of Richardson's involvement with Tibet. He spent longer in the city than any other foreigner in the first half of the twentieth century and spoke 'impeccable Lhasa Tibetan with a slight Oxford accent'.[40] As a member of the Gould Mission, Richardson often accompanied Spencer Chapman on his forays around Lhasa where the more experienced photographer (Chapman) avidly sought out the most advantageous spots from which to photograph the city. This kind of activity was often carried out on Sundays which were 'kept as a holiday' by the Christian Brits even when in Tibet. For example on 27 September 1936, the *Mission Diary* notes that Morgan, Chapman, Nepean and Richardson climbed a mountain 'of 17,450 ft. overlooking Drepung monastery' where photographs were taken. Spencer Chapman's depiction of the Potala seen from one

Hugh Richardson on Gyamberi
Frederick Spencer Chapman, 1936–1937

Hugh Richardson surrounded by lhato *(cairns dedicated to the gods) on the track near the summit of Gyamberi, a mountain not far from Lhasa. Richardson and Spencer Chapman climbed this mountain in order to take photographs of Lhasa below.*
PRM 1998.131.263.

of these vantage points, the Chakpori (the hill of the Lhasa Medical College), has become iconic, due to the brilliance of its composition, the significance of its subject matter and because the image of the Dalai Lama's palace has in the foreground another key signifier of Tibetan-ness – the practice of Tibetan Buddhist monks (shown playing horns – *rag dung*). The clarity of light in this image also adds to its appeal, and to achieve this Spencer Chapman made the ascent of Chakpori in the early morning.[41] The ethnographic evidence for this is visible in the image, for *rag dung* are sounded just after first light in all Tibetan Buddhist monasteries. The *Mission Diary* also chronicles Chapman's need to work at his photography at the beginning of the day when the air was relatively clear and shadows sharpened the contrast in his compositions.

The fact that thousands of photographs of the Potala have since been taken from the same position adopted by the British (such as the Potala from Chakpori) indicates the elision between outsiders and insiders perceptions of Tibet and the nodal points where the shared values of the two groups collide. I am suggesting that just as Bishop, Lopez and others have documented the degree to which Tibet has been imagined as a place whose cultural geography is dominated by Tibetan Buddhism, so the visual record of Tibet (and especially Lhasa) has been framed according to particular ways of seeing forged by the Anglo-Tibetan encounter. For British photographers in the 1930s and 1940s, the Tibetan landscape presented itself to them as one marked by religious buildings and bounded by massive mountains.[42] Their selection of scenic views was, in part, determined by British landscape aesthetics (dating back to Burke and the concept of the sublime in the 18th century) via the celebration of nature dramatised by the Romantic poets. However, British scholar-officials such as Bell, Richardson and Gould, also sought to comprehend Tibetan attitudes to place and space.[43] As we have noted above, the British focused on the same sites of power (whether religious or secular) which drew the attention of their hosts. The effectiveness of their attempts to map the socio-cultural world of Lhasa Tibetans can be gauged by the apparent familiarity of key sights in the city (such as a view of the Potala from Chakpori) in images of both pre- and post-1950 Lhasa.

However, as the primary photographer for the Gould Mission, Spencer Chapman also complained that, away from his mountainous observation posts, some parts of Lhasa did not emerge so readily for the camera. The Barkhor area, for example, presented a challenge, as the streets were narrow and cluttered by the activities of Tibetans.

The Potala Palace photographed from Chakpori
Frederick Spencer Chapman, 1936–1937

In the foreground, monks sound horns from the roof of the Tibetan Medical College at Chakpori. The Chakpori (Iron Hill) is considered to be one of Tibet's four most sacred mountains and the 5th Dalai Lama (1617–1682) had the medical college constructed there. The college combined the study of medicine and Buddhism. Photographers quickly discovered it to be an ideal vantage point from which to photograph the Potala Palace and the village of Shö. PRM 1998.131.305.

Lhasa Street Scene
Evan Nepean, 1936–1937

A group of Tibetan men, women and children in the Barkhor area watching the photographer Evan Nepean. A European (possibly Spencer Chapman) in suit and hat walks ahead. Note the Trilby hats worn by Tibetans.
PRM 2001.356.159.1.

The photographer simply could not get a good perspectival distance on his subject (such as the Jo khang).[44] When attempting to photograph the 13th Dalai Lama's memorial *chorten* (stupa) in the Potala, Chapman went so far as to complain that, because of the confined space (which prevented a 'comprehensive view'), the Tibetans should move the monument to a larger building. The smoke of 'innumerable dung fires' also obscured his vision, but Chapman develops a romantic sensibility in relation to this 'veil' of mist when he realises it also results from the Tibetan practice of burning juniper to propitiate the gods. Ultimately, British photographers such as Chapman had to accept that though it was no longer entirely 'forbidden' to them, Lhasa retained a kind of miasmic impenetrability, and that their viewing of it was conditional upon the support of their hosts. This theme is evident in photographs of ceremonies taken by several different British photographers over several years, but where the viewing point is clearly the same. For example, the Tibetans only allowed foreigners to witness events such as the Palden Lhamo procession from a balcony reserved for visitors overlooking the Jo khang.[45] Hence, though British intentions may have been directed by diplomatic, scientific and colonial archive ambitions, their representation of Tibet

The Trapchi Regiment riding through Central Lhasa
Harry Staunton, *c.* 1940–1942

During New Year's ceremonies, the cavalry of the Yasö generals ride through the streets of Lhasa on horseback. They are members of the Trapchi regiment based on the outskirts of Lhasa. Staunton photographed them from the vantage point of a balcony above the crowds.
PRM 1999.23.2.13.

was always mediated from particular intellectual, political and aesthetic vantage points which were to varying degrees determined by the values of their hosts. The resulting images therefore need to be viewed through a kind of double-frame of Tibetan and British ways of seeing.

Spencer Chapman preparing to Shoot Ciné Film
Evan Nepean, 1936

Spencer Chapman standing on wooden crates preparing to shoot portraits with one of his ciné cameras. Spencer Chapman spent a good deal of time setting up his shots and assessing how to achieve the best camera angle for the events and portraits he recorded. For example, during the Palden Lhamo ritual procession he set his cameras up on the roof of an artistocrat's house (the Surkhang mansion) which was located on the procession route. He also climbed the peaks around Lhasa in order to capture the city from above, and lamented that the Jo khang (the most sacred temple in Tibet) was too obscured by other buildings to get a good view of it.
PRM 2001.35.271.1.

Chapman admits that he literally saw Tibet through the filmic frame in his *Mission Diary* entry following the Regent's procession into Lhasa in 1936: 'Most of this incidentally was seen through the cinema camera's finder.' For Chapman not only took photographs, but also produced the first colour film footage of Lhasa (and he was often running three or four cameras at once).[46] He had established a reputation as an adventurer during two expeditions to Greenland (1930–31 and 1932–33) and as a pioneer of the visual with a film made there called 'Northen Lights'. The prospect of travelling to Tibet aroused dreams of reaching another remote location, coupled with the romance of Tibet-specific myths. In a lecture given to the Royal Photographic Society in London in 1937, he described his childhood ambition to reach the 'out of bounds places' of the world which he found so alluring. 'I often imagined myself disguised as a lama, riding a yak and turning a prayer wheel, of course, and going to the Forbidden City.'[47] No doubt these childish imaginings were only enriched by the published accounts of disguised Western travellers in Tibet such as Madame Alexandra David Néel (who published her *Voyage d'une Parisienne à Lhassa* in 1927) and William Montgomery McGovern (who published *To Lhasa in Disguise* in 1924, though he was much criticised by British officialdom for his secret, solo venture into Tibet),[48] but members of the Gould Mission would not have to enter into these charades – they would see, and be seen by, Tibetans without encumbrance. For Chapman, this provided the opportunity to produce a visual ethnography of Tibet which could compete with more fictionalised versions in circulation in Britain. Before he even reached Lhasa, Spencer Chapman was only too aware of the imaginative territory which had been claimed by James Hilton's best selling novel *Lost Horizon* (1933), the book which coined the term 'Shangri-La' and fixed a particular mythologised notion of Tibet in the public imagination. By 1937 Frank Capra's Hollywood version of *Lost Horizon* had been released, which seems to have riled Spencer Chapman since he begins his 1937 essay 'Tibetan Horizon' (about his own film-making in Tibet) with the immodest proposal that the producers of the film might have improved their product and 'saved themselves the inconvenience' of visiting Tibet by viewing the 'photographic results of Mr. B. J. Gould's recent diplomatic mission to Lhasa.'[49] Though Gould's predecessors (most notably Bell) had photographed Lhasa during their stay in the capital, the Gould Mission was charged with an explicit agenda to record the city in more detail than any previous British Mission.[50] Spencer Chapman clearly saw himself as the author of the most complete documentary account of Lhasa compared to which all other previous versions were inauthentic. In this, he was deemed to have succeeded by the *Times* film reviewer: 'The film's great achievement was to present, however ramblingly, a true vivid and sufficiently comprehensive picture of life in Lhasa, stripping its citizency (sic) of mumbo-jumbo and investing them, from the beggar to the Minister of State, with a slightly embarrassed reality, more suggestive than any amount of sensational legend. It must be admitted that the Potala and the great monastery of Drepeing (sic) recalled, even while they transcended, the architectural wishfulfilments of a Californian realtor which are to be seen in the film Lost Horizon.'[51] Though he regretted that his film of Tibet was 'without plot and without love interest',[52] Chapman hoped that it would be a box-office success and hence many of his activities on returning from Tibet in 1937 were dedicated towards replacing previous imaginings of Tibet (textual, but also and especially visual) with his own, officially-sanctioned representations. His public profile rose through a series of film showings, lectures and publications to the extent that he was immortalised as a cartoon character in the *TV Express* magazine, and in 1963 was sufficiently well-known to be the subject of the popular British television programme 'This is Your Life'.

In order to achieve this supposedly comprehensive coverage, a huge quantity of equipment was transported over the Himalayas (crossing passes of over 16,000 feet) on the backs of nearly 400 mules and yaks. The movement of this amount of cameras, film, generators and other gadgetry was made possible by marshalling the full

***This is Your Life* Frederick Spencer Chapman**
Photographer Unknown, 1963

A still from the BBC television programme 'This is Your Life' featuring the career of Frederick Spencer Chapman. Chapman (with his back to the camera) is shown greeting his old Tibet colleague Evan Nepean whilst his wife Faith and the presenter Eamon Andrews look on. One of his photographs of the Potala Palace appears as a studio backdrop behind them.
Courtesy of the BBC.
PRM 2001.35.393.

logistical force of the colonial infrastructure and stands as testimony to the status of Gould in the eyes of the British government whilst simultaneously providing him with what Hansen dubs a 'positional credibility'[53] in relation to the Tibetans. The apparatus of Empire was also required in order to release the full potential of Chapman's film shot in Tibet. During the six month mission, he took 13,000 feet of standard 35 mm film (all silent), 6,000 feet of 16 mm, Kodachrome colour film and 3,000 feet of 16 mm black-and-white which had to be sent to London via Calcutta for processing.[54] Spencer Chapman then edited the results in the Dekyi Lingka 'On one occasion I had 2 miles of 35 mm film carefully cut and hanging in lengths from the wires I had rigged up at one end of our dining-room.'[55] He took nine cameras in all (4 ciné and 5 still) and managed to develop 2,500 still photographs in Lhasa as the local water proved suitable for the task 'if strained through a handkerchief'.[56] All of this activity was designed to assert the visibility of an official British Mission both within Tibet and to the wider world of the British Empire beyond.

Photographs by Spencer Chapman and other members of the Mission, such as Evan Nepean, Hugh Richardson and Colonel Philip Neame, were collected into albums and sent back to the hub of Empire in London with the official Mission Diary reports on a weekly basis.[57] Unlike some earlier accounts such as Perceval Landon's *Lhasa* – which was illustrated with watercolours and drawings made after the event or with photographs of objects held in British museums, the 1936 Mission could mobilise photography as a tool for attesting that the journey had been made and that the diplomatic objectives had been achieved in the process. This wider agenda is evident in Basil Gould's use of film of the 14th Dalai Lama's Installation, supposedly shot in secret 'from behind a garden wall' in Lhasa in 1940. In 1944, Gould showed this material to a London audience including representatives of the Ministry of Information and the Foreign and India Offices. Afterwards, a member of the audience is said to have remarked: 'It would do the Americans a lot of good to see the film of Tibet; it should help to convince them that Tibet is not a part of China.'[58] In general, Gould was keen to do all he could to present Tibet as an independent country by emphasising such things as a distinctive art tradition and other markers of cultural uniqueness.[59] His successor, Hugh Richardson took this objective even more to heart by assiduously documenting the historic monuments of Tibet during

Preparations for the Installation of the 14th Dalai Lama
Harry Staunton, 1940

In 1940, Staunton and Gould were the only two Westerners to witness the Installation of the 14th Dalai Lama in the Potala Palace in Lhasa. As the Tibetans enforced a strict protocol over who could attend and when, they were only allowed to be present on the second day of the ceremony. In this image, a group of officials are gathered next to the Dalai Lama's throne prior to the ceremony. They include the Chief Engineer of Sikkim (in a turban) third from left.
PRM 1999.23.2.30.

Man making Notes on a *Doring*
Hugh Richardson, c. 1936–1950

Hugh Richardson's Tibetan assistant making notes of inscriptions on the Karchung doring *(pillar) at Ramagang near Lhasa.*
PRM 2001.59.17.60.1.

A Lunch Party (opposite)
Harry Staunton, *c.* 1940–1942

While in Lhasa, the members of the British Mission were invited to numerous parties where huge quantities of food were served by Tibetan hosts. While it is unclear exactly which party is recorded here, the man at the far end of the table can be identified as Rai Bahadur Norbhu Dhondhup who was an 'attached' member of the British Political department. Sikkimese by birth, he was given the high rank of Dzasa by the 13th Dalai Lama (1876–1933) for his help with British-Tibetan relations. Hence he was permitted to wear the elaborate clothing seen here. He was awarded a CBE and an OBE by the British for his work at the Lhasa Mission. Gould notes that the only time he ever saw Norbhu upset was when it was pointed out that it was not the done thing to wear the two awards at the same time.
PRM 1999.23.1.2.4.

the eight years he spent in the country. He travelled beyond Lhasa to some of the earliest sites of Tibetan culture such as the Yarlung valley, the monastery of Samye and photographed as many *doring* (pillars inscribed with treaties) and *chorten* as he could. These efforts later provided invaluable material for Richardson's publications on Tibetan history produced on his return to the United Kingdom and which have made him perhaps the best known British scholar-official of Tibet.

Portraits and Parties

For the 1936 Mission the primary diplomatic aim had been simply to stay there longer than any previous group of European visitors and in so doing to provide a competing presence against the Chinese in Lhasa. Hence great emphasis was placed on recording the degree to which the British became embedded in the social order of Lhasa. Consulting the Mission Diaries, we get the

impression of a round of social engagements almost as hectic as those depicted in a novel by Jane Austen – lunches, dinners, audiences and parties were assiduously reciprocated by both sides (and this atmosphere of conviviality was preserved, as far as possible, by Hugh Richardson on Gould's departure). Characterising himself as the 'portraitist' to the 1936 Mission, Spencer Chapman made concerted attempts to photograph all the key players Gould encountered. His depiction of members of the Lhasa nobility, the holders of government posts and religious leaders, therefore often have the deliberate air and style of British portrait painting in the manner established in the eighteenth century. Subjects have clearly been posed and arranged for the camera with careful attention paid to the fabric (literally) of the environment they occupy. Hence Kunga Wangchuk Langdün, nephew of the 13th Dalai Lama and Prime Minister of Tibet, is captured sitting with his wife and child in bejewelled finery against a backdrop of Chinese silk and Central Asian carpets. Their solemn pose is tinged with a proprietorial confidence akin to Thomas Gainsborough's painting of Mr and Mrs Andrews at their

Kyibu Wangdu Norbhu and His Wife
Frederick Spencer Chapman, 1936–1937

Kyibu, a 6th rank official in charge of the city police, with his wife. Kyibu was married to one of Jigme Taring's sisters and lived in a house near the Jo khang. He was one of four boys sent to England to be educated at Rugby in 1913 (arranged by Sir Charles Bell and the 13th Dalai Lama). On his return to Lhasa he was put in charge of developing the telegraph system, which he knew little about, and so he soon retired to the family estates. Spencer Chapman describes him as a 'nervous little man with an apologetic air and a straggly moustache'. (1938:86)
PRM 1998.131.497.

The Prime Minister of Tibet – Yabzhi Langdün Kunga Wangchuk with his wife and daughter
(previous page)
Frederick Spencer Chapman, 1936–1937

The Prime Minister of Tibet, Yabzhi Langdün, at home with his wife and daughter. Spencer Chapman describes Gould's first meeting with him: 'He was not very easy to get on with, and remained very much the official, seated on a ceremonial divan at a higher level than the one he had prepared for Gould.' The Mission members attributed his stiffness to 'youth and inexperience, rather than to any feeling of unfriendliness'. (1938:101–2) Langdün was the nephew of the 13th Dalai Lama (1876–1933), which might explain why he acquired such an important job at the young age of 26. He was greatly concerned with status and would demand a film show at his house if somebody else had already had one. He commissioned Spencer Chapman to produce this family portrait.
PRM 1998.131.437.

Suffolk estate. However, this family portrait was commissioned by the Prime Minister himself – hence we may assume a certain amount of agency on the part of the Tibetan subjects: it may well be that they chose the setting for this image and thereby determined how they were to be represented to contemporary and future viewers. Portraying themselves surrounded by valuable textiles indicates their economic status and access to trade networks across Asia.

Though the circumstances for another portrait, that of Sonam Rabten (the Minister of Agriculture in 1936), may have been similar, the compositional devices used to portray him (similarly resplendent in silk and seated on tiger skins) have the effect of somehow neutralising the force of the subject's personality under the weight of an aestheticising regard. The staticity of the image somewhat contradicts the reported ebullience of the minister's character. Chapman knew him as: 'The champion beer drinker of all Tibet.' Reting Rinpoche, who served as Regent of Tibet following the death of the 13th Dalai Lama, is repeatedly photographed by Chapman who at first seems to want to emphasise the fragility of the monk's physique.[60] Witness the image where he appears with his minder, a massive monk (nick-named 'Simple Simon' by the British) and two bird cages.[61] As in other formal portraits of the Regent, the young man is presented as a caged creature himself and overburdened by the weight of his responsibilities. Chapman described him in the *Mission Diary* as, 'a frail, undersized, almost emaciated looking monk of about twenty three years of age, with very prominent ears. He has a receding chin and peculiar creases above the bridge of his nose which when he frowns assume the shape of rudimentary horns.' We can demonstrate the selectivity involved in Chapman's view of this subject by comparison with an image made at the same time from the collection of Evan Nepean (but probably, in fact, made by Neame). In this

Sonam Rabten, the Minister of Agriculture (opposite)
Frederick Spencer Chapman, 1936–1937

Sonam Rabten had been the Mipön (Mayor) of Lhasa in the 1920s and became the Tibetan Minister of Agriculture in 1936. As an ex-army man, he often talked to the British and specifically Colonel Neame about the Tibetan military situation. In 1939 Rabten was part of the official reception party for Tenzin Gyatso upon his recognition as the 14th Dalai Lama. Spencer Chapman recorded his impressions of the man thus: 'Once seen, [he] is not easily forgotten, being the very embodiment of Falstaff. He is of enormous size, and is perpetually out of breath and perspiring. His face is continuously wreathed in smiles, and he is the champion drinker of chang in all Tibet, having the rare and enviable accomplishment of being able to pour a glass of beer straight down his throat without swallowing.' (1938:84)
PRM 1998.131.499.

photograph, another monk is included in the scene whereas Spencer Chapman crops him out of the frame to increase the sense of contrasting body types.

The Regent of Tibet with 'Simple Simon'
Frederick Spencer Chapman, 1936–1937

The Regent of Tibet, Reting Rinpoche (seated), with a monk body guard known to the British as 'Simple Simon'. According to Spencer Chapman, during this photographic session, 'when we all went into the garden the Regent had no objection to being photographed, and it was all I could do to persuade his huge orderly (whom we nicknamed Simple Simon) to move about when I wanted to take some cinema films; he struck what he thought was an imposing attitude and resolutely refused to move.' In the 1936 Mission Diaries 'Simple Simon' appears again when on 28 August 1937 the Mission members called upon the Regent at his home: 'Neame and Chapman were allowed to take photos and ciné of the Regent; amongst his attendants was a giant lama, some 7-feet high, and when Neame snapped him he began to talk and wave his arms. These were not threatening gestures as he was only asking for a copy of the photo.'
PRM 1998.131.522.

Hugh Richardson's portraits of the Regent are also relatively formal, though his photographs of other subjects provide a more intimate record of relationships established over the eight years he spent in Tibet. Amongst the Pitt Rivers Museum collection of Richardson prints and negatives, at least one hundred record key religious and secular figures, and many prints are inscribed on the reverse with the name of the sitter in transliterated Tibetan. Richardson clearly benefited from his long stay in Lhasa and his proficiency in the language, for his photography suggests that he enjoyed exceptional access to members of the religious elite, such as the Nechung Oracle – described by Richardson as a 'personal friend' (but a figure Chapman did not catch on camera). Many of Richardson's pictures reflect the increasing ease with which some Tibetans approached the British and their cameras, as is evident in his shot of the Regent's half brother Gyaltsen Yuton Sumdowa on a swing in a Lhasa garden or his picture of a relaxed group of Tibetan men in a tent (probably taken at a picnic party). This kind of photography has a noticeably different tone and style to the imaging of Tibetans carried out in the past by British cadres such as Bell. The latter's emphasis on hieratic, symmetrically posed subjects (partly determined by the technology of the time) is gradually eclipsed by a more decentred and relaxed depiction of the Tibetans encountered

Sumdowa on a Swing
Hugh Richardson, *c.* 1936–1950

The 4th rank official Gyaltsen Yuton Sumdowa on a swing in a Lhasa garden. Sumdowa was the half-brother of the Nechung Oracle, Lobzang Namgye. An unknown European observes.
PRM 2001.59.12.23.1.

The Nechung Oracle in His Garden
Hugh Richardson, *c.* 1936–1945

The State Oracle of Tibet, who plays a key role in predicting future events and identifying reincarnations of the Dalai Lama, photographed in his garden at Nechung monastery. Richardson gave the following description of him: 'When Sir Basil Gould visited Lhasa in 1936 the Nechung Oracle, to general surprise came to visit him. Such a meeting had never happened before. He was a sturdy monk with a large, smiling, rather pale face and an open and cheerful manner who later became a very good and hospitable friend. He was about forty-two years old and his name was Lobzang Namgye. He had formerly been a junior official in the Shö office, known to be sociable and very fond of mahjong. In 1934 without warning and much against his will he was chosen for the position and became a greatly venerated personage with the title of Ta Lama and the honorific epithet of Chöjé and the duties of a Chökyong, a protector of the faith, and the head of a small wealthy monastery with a pleasant sunny house of his own. During my time at Lhasa before his death in 1945, whenever I left or returned there officially, I would find his steward waiting by the side of the road with an urgent command to go up to Nechung for tea with the Ta Lama, which always included a delicious lunch. At other times I visited him in his country estate in the Tölung valley where he and his monks relaxed in a pleasant park, wearing holiday dress and enjoying archery at which the Oracle was expert. In return he came frequently to Dekyilingka often at short notice.' (1993:49–50)
PRM 2001.59.18.12.1.

by his successors. This process is also evident in Spencer Chapman's Lhasa pictures, as they increasingly reflect the familiarity engendered by frequent meetings with Tibetans in more informal settings. Social and cultural boundaries are shown to be subject to a kind of slippage, particularly in the context of technological and ludic innovations. Over time, Chapman's view of the Regent for example, has demonstrably altered. On the occasion of Reting's initiation into the

The Regent of Tibet at a Microphone
Frederick Spencer Chapman, 1936–1937

The Regent of Tibet, Reting Rinpoche, seated at a microphone with Norbhu Dhondhup (far right) and Dasang Damdul Tsarong (far left) amongst the Tibetans looking on. For this occasion, Evan Nepean and Sidney Dagg set up a public-address amplifier and a gramophone player in the Regent's garden.
PRM 1998.131.520.

thrills of a public address system and gramophone player (which the British had brought to the garden of his house), Chapman notes: 'Nothing but the loudest possible noise would satisfy the regent. Later he went and spoke into the microphone himself, at first rather self consciously, but gradually found great amusement in the sound of his own words voice booming back at him.'[62] His photographs of this encounter are therefore framed in a new way, acknowledging a more extrovert, sociable dimension in the Regent's character – and a more accurate reflection of Tibetan views of a man whose personal life was undoubtedly passionate.

Looking at images of Lhasa in the 1930s and 1940s allows us to explore the complex nexus of social relations between Tibetans and the British on the cusp of Empire. The photographic and textual record of British Missions to Lhasa illustrate the meeting of two elites who saw much to admire in each other; particularly those things which seemed oddly familiar. Both the Tibetans and the British attached high value to hierarchy, etiquette, gift giving and sophisticated dinner parties. Basil Gould insisted on respecting both British and Tibetan standards of decorum – hence his Mission halted some miles outside Lhasa for an official Tibetan welcoming party before venturing into the city and thereafter spent many hours waiting for Tibetan guests to arrive at the Dekyi Lingka. As the *Mission Diary* for 1 January 1937 notes: 'In Tibet as in other countries, the more important a man is the later he can afford to be.' Hierarchical dress codes were also strictly adhered to by both groups when attending religious and

Jigme Taring in New Year Dress
Frederick Spencer Chapman, 1937

Jigme Taring in gyaluche, *robes and ornaments of the Yarlung dynasty rulers of Tibet (7th–9th centuries AD), which were only worn at ceremonies such as New Year. Jigme was the nephew of Raja Taring of Sikkim and had attended St Paul's school in Darjeeling, India. In 1936, he was a Depön (general in the Tibetan army). Jigme later became a member of the Tibetan government and the chief architect in Lhasa. He also married Rinchen Dolma ('Mary') Taring, with whom he lived in a small house next to the Tsarong family mansion. Both he and his wife spoke fluent English and were friendly with the members of the British Mission. After 1959, he continued to work for the Tibetan government-in-exile whilst his wife founded the Tibetan Homes Foundation in Mussorie, Northern India.*
PRM 1998.131.492.

Sir Basil J. Gould (opposite)
Frederick Spencer Chapman, 1936–1937

Sir Basil J. Gould in full dress uniform. The Political Officer for Sikkim, Bhutan and Tibet and leader of the 1936 British Mission to Lhasa, Gould was invited to attend the installation of the 14th Dalai Lama in 1940 and made a final visit to Tibet in 1944. Heavily influenced by Sir Charles Bell (one of his predecessors as Political Officer), Gould was determined to establish a firm foothold for the British government in Tibet. He also took great pains to record and translate the Tibetan language, and is said to have memorised a set of stock honorific phrases to assist in his diplomatic endeavours. As a career diplomat he was highly conscious of status, within both the British and Tibetan systems. He was pleased to be referred to as Lönchen – equating his rank with that of a Tibetan Prime Minister and is reputed to have worn evening dress for dinner even when in camp.
PRM 1998.131.388.

Three Shapé of the Tibetan Cabinet (Kashag)
Frederick Spencer Chapman, 1936–1937

The four members of the Tibetan Cabinet are known as Shapé. Those photographed here are, from left to right: Tenthong, Bhonthong and Lancunga. They wear the turquoise ear-rings (sog gil) *and yellow silk gowns of high-ranking lay officials. Spencer Chapman describes those present: 'Tendong Shap-pe was Depon [General] in Kham for many years and has the reputation of being a great fighter … Bhondong Shap-pe … has a fat face, with a ready grin, and a moustache drooping over the corners of his mouth like a mandarin. As he was for many years secretary to the Cabinet, and successfully won his way to his present position, he has a great knowledge of the Lhasa methods of government … Langchungna … is very conservative, continually saying that Lhasa is not what it was when he was boy, especially with regard to the weather, the deterioration of which, he declares, coincided with the installation of electric light. He says that wireless and electric light have made the winters stuffy. Nobody quite knows why he was made a Shap-pe, as he is neither of noble family nor of conspicuous brilliance.' (1938:75) Spencer Chapman also noted that Lancunga did not like cameras and would scowl whenever anybody tried to take a picture of him.*
PRM 1998.157.96.

state ceremonials, with Gould as resplendent in full military uniform as his Tibetan counterparts. The Tibetans were observed to have an equally complex system of marking social rank by sartorial means – with head-gear, jewellery and fabrics all indicating prestige (or the lack of it). For example, only lay members of the Kashag ruling body or cabinet (who were known as Shapé) wore gold silk *chuba* (a long coat). Lower-ranking Tibetans wore less flamboyant colours, paralleling the British practice which saw Richardson and Chapman in morning coats. Dining also promoted intercultural exchange as the Tibetans and British vied with one another to produce the longest, most complex and exotic meals, though clearly (as with much else) perceptions of strangeness were culture-specific. For the British, yak tongue and shark's stomach were challenges to the palate, whilst the Tibetans were treated to the novelty of Bully beef.

These moments of mirroring, when Tibetans and Britishers were able to examine one another at close quarters were often photographed by those who attended. Spencer Chapman seems to have made a habit of setting up his camera at the end of Lhasa dining tables and other members of the Mission followed his example to make snaps of themselves at play with Tibetans. (Harry Staunton sent home a picture of himself with his Tibetan assistant labelled 'We have a plentiful supply of beer' on the reverse.) The attractive female servants who playfully forced the diners to drink Tibetan beer (*chang*) on these occasions became a popular subject for all photographers (official or unofficial, of high and low rank) as this may have been the closest many British men came to contact with Tibetan women.[63] These women were

Harry Staunton and Tonyot Tsering at the Dekyi Lingka
Reginald Fox (?), May 1940

Dr Harry Staunton and Dr Tonyot Tsering smoking and drinking on the steps of the Dekyi Lingka (the British Mission house in Lhasa). Staunton wears Tibetan dress and Tonyot is in Western attire. Staunton was the Civil Surgeon for Bhutan and Tibet from 1940–1942 and the Sikkimese Rai Sahib Tonyot Tsering was his sub-assistant surgeon (S.A.S.). All the British doctors in Lhasa had non-British assistants, no doubt partly to ensure that someone could speak to the patients in Tibetan. The inscription by Staunton on the reverse of this photograph is: 'S.A.S. and self. We have a good supply of beer! Lhasa May 1940'. On this occasion the beer seems to be of the British kind rather than the Tibetan chang.
PRM 1999.23.2.65.

British Mission Members with Tibetan Officials (opposite)
Evan Nepean, 1936

From left to right: Colonel Philip Neame, Hugh Richardson, a member of the Tibetan government, a monk official and Norbhu Dhondhup (advisor to the Mission) in a Lhasa street. A group of servants look on from the entrance to an aristocratic house. Richardson had served as British Trade Agent at Yatung, but joined the 1936 Gould Mission to Lhasa and served as representative of the British Government when Gould left in 1947. Colonel Neame's role in the 1936 Mission was to assess the military capabilities of the Tibetans. Though his report on the Tibetan army was scathing, he spent a great deal of time in Lhasa discussing potential improvements with Tibetan officials.
PRM 2001.35.218.1.

The British Mission of 1936 Lunch with the Lord Chamberlain
Frederick Spencer Chapman, 1936–1937

The British Mission lunch with the Chikyab Khenpo (Lord Chamberlain of Tibet). From left to right: Sidney Dagg, Evan Nepean, the Lord Chamberlain, Dr. William Morgan, Sir Basil Gould. At this particular meal the delicacies included sea slugs, sharks fin and Jacobs crackers. Members of the Mission are shown eating with chopsticks as was the practice of high-ranking Tibetans.
PRM 1998.131.413.

Spencer Chapman Photographing an Outdoor Party
Evan Nepean, 1936

Spencer Chapman recorded much of the social interaction between Tibetans and the British during the 1936 Mission to Lhasa. Here Nepean shows him with his camera set up at an outdoor lunch party attended by members of the Mission, Tibetan dignitaries (including monks) and 'chang *(Tibetan beer) girls'. Since Spencer Chapman often worked with several cameras at once, Evan Nepean assisted him and also took his own photographs. See below.*
PRM 2001.35.351.1.

An Outdoor Lunch Party
Frederick Spencer Chapman, 1936–1937

A party (probably in the garden of the Dekyi Lingka) attended by members of the British Mission including Evan Nepean cupping his hands and calling to someone across the table. These parties were often particularly raucous due to the presence of the so-called 'chang *girls'.*
PRM 2001.35.355.1.

Women and Children of the Tsarong Household
Frederick Spencer Chapman, 1936–1937

From left to right: Rinchen Dolma (later 'Mary' Taring), Pema Dolkar and Norbhu Yudon with three children. The women are sisters, daughters of the previous head of the Tsarong family who was killed along with his son for alleged support of the Chinese army that invaded in 1910. When Dasang Damdul Tsarong married the son's widow (Rigzin Choden), he took over as head of the family and adopted their name. However, the people of the Tsarong estate worried that this might mean the end of the bloodline, so Tsarong also married the eldest daughter Pema Dolkar. He later also married Rinchen Dolma and a younger sister (not seen here) Tseten Dolkar, the widow of another Tibetan aristocrat, Horkhang. Norbhu Yudon was married into the Dele Rabden family. British reactions to these women were varied: Rinchen Dolma was said to speak perfect English, Mrs Dele Rabden was described as distinguished looking but shy, and Pema Dolkar as the perfect hostess.
PRM 1998.131.479.

traditionally allowed to dispense with some of the strictures of Tibetan etiquette and to even prod the most estimable guests (including the Prime Minister) with a pin. The impact of the so-called '*chang* girls' was so great that they featured in Basil Gould's report on the Mission published in the London *Times* and in photographic form in Chapman's *Lhasa: the Holy City*. The fact that Evan Nepean inscribed the reverse of his photograph of a Lhasa party with the words '*tunda nang ro nang*' ('please drink, drink') suggests that these social encounters even provided a small opportunity for members of the British party to learn some Tibetan. This access to women was interpreted by the British as a sign of the congeniality of Tibetan culture in a more general sense and was a factor which differed from the situation in India (as noted by Richardson in his report on the 1936 Mission). Though Spencer Chapman found that women street traders in the Barkhor were reluctant to be photographed, he had little difficulty in working with aristocrats such as Mary (Rinchen Dolma) Taring, but she had been educated in Darjeeling and had already been photographed in a studio there in 1923.[64] Thus, photography was not a complete revelation for some high-ranking Tibetans, and attitudes towards it were determined by class as much as by gender.

'*Chang* Girls'
Evan Nepean, 1936

*Portrait of the women who served Tibetan beer (*chang*) at the party given by the British Mission for the Shapés of the Tibetan Cabinet (Kashag). The so-called '*chang *girls' at these official parties were usually servants from leading Lhasa aristocratic families who could also be commandeered to work for the Tibetan government. Their role was to pour out *chang *and cajole party-goers (by fair means or foul) to empty their glasses. One girl would pour beer from an enamel teapot while another kept her supplied from a larger container. Spencer Chapman often describes them as being 'remarkably pretty'. In this portrait, the women have decorated their faces with gum as beauty spots.*
PRM 2001.35.358.

Hugh Richardson attended by a '*Chang* Girl'
Frederick Spencer Chapman, 1936–1937

This photograph records the occasion when the British Mission entertained the Shapés of the Tibetan Cabinet (Kashag) in the garden of the Dekyi Lingka. Dr. Morgan had to fend off the chang *girls with a soda siphon.*
PRM 1998.131.680.

Protracted social interaction with Tibetans was considered conducive to building lasting friendly relations at a diplomatic level between Britain and Tibet, even if one of the vehicles for this engagement, football, meant that the Tibetans never scored a goal. (The local teams complained that the British had an unfair advantage in their 'fearful boots' and threatened to stop playing unless they were equally well shod. Before this issue could be resolved the games ceased altogether when someone extracted the goal posts for firewood; *Mission Diary*, 9 November 1936.) During the 1936 Mission a number of very British games were introduced to Tibet including a paper-chase 'hunt' by 'Mr. Gould's Hounds' (i.e. members of the Mission on horseback), which was frequently disrupted by the Tibetan habit of picking up the scraps of paper marking the trail as Spencer Chapman noted in the *Mission Diary* for 2 November 1936. 'The Tibetans, by the way, could not understand what we had lost'. The invention of two football teams – 'Lhasa United' (a team mainly comprised of Ladakhi Muslims and Nepalis but sometimes augmented by women such as Mary Taring) representing Tibet and the 'Mission Marmots' (made up of members of the Mission with Gould often taking the role of goal keeper) representing Britain, emphasises the sense in which the ludic was seen as a useful diplomatic tool in Anglo-Tibetan relations.[65]

Drinking Party at the Dekyi Lingka
Evan Nepean, 1936

This photograph is inscribed by Nepean on the reverse with the phrase 'tunda nang-ro-nang' *('please drink, drink'). The consumption of* chang *seems to have helped the British to learn some Tibetan.*
PRM 2001.35.382.

The 'Mission Marmots' Football Team
Frederick Spencer Chapman,
1936–1937

'The Mission Marmots' was the name given to the 1936 British Mission football team. The Mission established this team to play against various local groups (including 'Lhasa United') on a pitch beyond the Norbulingka. No goal was ever conceded by the British, perhaps because they wore army field boots. The football season came to an abrupt end when someone stole the goalposts to use for firewood and sandstorms became frequent. Team members (back row from left to right): Sonam, unknown person, Minghu; (middle row from left to right): Frederick Spencer Chapman, Sidney Dagg, Dr. William Morgan, Evan Nepean; (bottom row) unidentified Mission assistants.
PRM 1998.131.384.

The 'Lhasa United' Football Team
Frederick Spencer Chapman,
1936–1937

Members of the 'Lhasa United' football team. Spencer Chapman describes a match against 'Lhasa United' in October 1936: 'Together with a crowd of supporters, our opponents were already there, turned out in garish harlequin-coloured silk shirts with L.U. sewn on to the pockets. They were a remarkable looking team, and certainly needed to be "United"! There was a tough looking Nepali soldier, a Chinese tailor, three bearded Ladakhis wearing red fezes – the most hirsute being the goalkeeper, a Sikkimese clerk of Pangda-Tsang's, and five Tibetan officials, including our friends Yuto, Surkang-Se, and Taring Dzongpon. The latter still had their charm-boxes on top of their heads, so were precluded from heading the ball.' (1938:269)
PRM 1998.131.385.

Game of Football outside Lhasa
Frederick Spencer Chapman, 1936–1937

A game of football between 'Lhasa United' and the 'Mission Marmots' in progress. The ground was two miles beyond the Norbulingka in a sandy area surrounded by thorn thickets. Spencer Chapman remarks that 'Playing at 12,000 feet above sea-level is not so much of an ordeal as one would imagine, though sometimes one would rush down the field and find oneself quite unable to breathe. Then it was necessary to lie down for a few moments in the middle of the field until one's breath returned.' (1938:270) The match was apparently a 'good clean game'.
PRM 1998.131.386.

Lunch Party at the Dekyi Lingka
Harry Staunton, *c.* 1940–1942

This appears to be a lunch at the British Mission house, the Dekyi Lingka, as the walls are decorated with posters advertising tourist sites (such as the Taj Mahal) in British India. From left to right are Reginald Fox, Norbhu Dhondhup, Basil Gould, an unidentified Tibetan monk and Phünkang Shapé. Reginald Fox was the telegraphist for the Mission during the 1940s and married a Tibetan woman during his stay in Lhasa. Rai Bahadur Norbhu Dhondhup was an 'attached' member of the British Political Department. Basil Gould was the head of the British Mission in Lhasa in 1936. Phünkang was both a member of the Tibetan government and known to the British as 'The Duke' (Kung), since he descended from the family of one of the Dalai Lamas.
PRM 1999.23.1.22.1.

However, the most explicit example of such manipulation of a well-established British cultural practice to suit the Tibetan situation is found in the use of film. Gould was not the first to introduce cinema to Lhasa. By 1920, the Tibetans had discovered it for themselves, as Bell reports viewing films at the Tsarong house in Lhasa. Frederick Williamson had shown his own footage alongside newsreel of London in 1933, but three years later Gould took his predecessor's idea of inserting a little 'mild propaganda'[66] to another level. As we have noted, Spencer Chapman was charged with the task of filming all that the eye surveyed in Lhasa. He also edited the film until 'it was fit to be shown to our discriminating audiences'.[67] The Mission then invited a select group of their Tibetan friends to be entertained at the Dekyi Lingka with a mixture of Charlie Chaplin and Rin Tin Tin movies, scenes of royal ceremonial and other aspects of life in Britain and the film shot in Tibet, though the audience often swelled with gate-crashers – including monks. Most film-shows opened with this actualité footage, as both Gould and Chapman observed that seeing themselves on film encouraged Tibetans to suspend their disbelief in the face of the moving image.[68] This initiation into a Western system of seeing was vital, for it ensured that Tibetans would comprehend the reality of the views of Britain which followed. They were treated to the Hendon Air Show (1929), the Grand National, the King's Jubilee Procession in London and other scenes emphasising the sophistication of British life. The Tibetans were reported to be suitably impressed by the cleanliness of London streets and the grandeur of St Paul's cathedral (a British equivalent to the Potala or Jo khang?). Comparisons between the pomp and circumstance of the British monarchy and Tibetan ceremonial were inevitable. The Gould Mission was both turning the lens onto the Tibetans and reflecting those markers of Britishness which would be most in tune with Tibetan values. Hence the effect was not perhaps so much to stamp an impression of cultural superiority over the Tibetans, as to provide further evidence of the ways in which Britishness and Tibetaness could mirror one another. When commenting on the popularity of the feature films – with their slapstick humour and canine protagonists, Gould remarked that 'Tibetans laugh at just the same things and in the same tone, and appreciate beauty in just the same things as Englishmen.'[69]

Exchange and the Photographic Gift

The Dekyi Lingka film shows became a highlight of the Lhasa social calendar and once they had seen themselves on screen, Tibetans regularly asked for prints (Chapman calls them 'enlargements') of themselves and their families. Since Chapman was able to develop his pictures *in situ*, he could also deliver them to his 'customers' within the social world of Lhasa. Thus

Potala Palace New Year Card
Made by Dasang Damdul Tsarong and sent to Basil Gould 1937

The Potala Palace photographed by Tsarong from the east side and attached to daphne bark paper as a New Year card. This one was signed and sent to Sir Basil Gould in Lhasa in 1937. Private Collection.

photographs functioned as agents confirming networks of social cohesion.[70] Like the *kula* valuables of the Trobriand Islanders, so famously described by Malinowski, photographic objects circulated amongst Tibetans in Lhasa accruing value and resonance and enhancing the status of their owners. (A precursor for this movement exists in Tibet in the form of the widespread distribution of photo-icons of the 13th Dalai Lama and other religious figures.)[71] This was also the case for the British who clearly shared the results of their photographic forays in Lhasa. As participants in a British Mission, any object acquired during the trip was officially the property of the Government and hence should be deposited in an appropriate institution such as the India Office at the heart of Empire in London.[72] It seems that photographs were also subject to this regulation – hence Spencer Chapman refers to his work as 'the photographic results of Mr B J Gould's recent diplomatic mission to Lhasa'. Other mission photographers presented their material for incorporation into the Mission Diary that was sent back to London each week. In the final compendium of text, the photographs are referred to numerically but no acknowledgement is made to individual photographers.

An album of mission photographs (labelled *Lhasa 1936*) was presented to the India Office and leading members of the Mission on their return along with a copy of the Mission Diary.[73] Once again the photographs were presented as the product of a collective exercise and the albums do not contain information about who took which picture. If we consult the seven draft albums made in Tibet (on loan to the Pitt Rivers Museum), it is equally difficult to disentangle the work of one photographer from another. (A problem exacerbated by the fact that Chapman must have processed other people's pictures whilst in Lhasa.) However, by amassing the negatives from several members of the Mission and consulting their collections of prints we can begin to identify different hands (and eyes) at work.[74] We can also observe the ways in which certain images escaped the official canon, and retained a more intimate flavour by comparing official and private albums such as those produced by Evan Nepean and Harry Staunton. In his personal album, Nepean includes a photograph of his good friend Chapman in the Kyi Chu river alongside one of himself in an identical position and posture so that they appear like happy twin boys on a school outing. The same pictures were stuck onto Tibetan paper in a draft album assembled in Lhasa but never made it into the official visual record presented to the Government and the Mission leaders. (Though many others were used as the raw material for publication purposes, as the multi-coloured marking and excisions

Three Tibetan Women in a Tent
Harry Staunton, *c.* 1940–1942

Three female members of the Lhasa aristocracy seated on chairs with their young children sitting crosslegged at their feet. The caption written by Staunton on the reverse reads: 'Tibetan Glamour Girls.'
PRM 1999.23.2.63.

in the draft albums suggest. See, for example, Chapman's pictures used to illustrate Frederick O'Connor's 1937 essay 'Tibet in the Modern World' [published in the *Geographical Magazine*] where Chapman is said to have taken the pictures 'on behalf of' the Gould Mission.) Hundreds of small prints were passed between members of the Mission and some were recycled to function as postcards sent to family back home with a short missive written on their reverse. These pictures transfer us into the domain of individual narratives revealing sentiments which may have been impossible to voice amongst the rambunctious camaraderie of British (mainly military) men on a posting overseas. A 1940 photograph of Harry Staunton resting on a high pass on his way out of Tibet is inscribed 'Feeling a little blue'. However, another describes his photograph of three matronly women as 'Tibetan glamour girls'.

The ability of a photographic print to perform the role of a postcard in which information is communicated to a recipient can also be inverted, allowing the image to be a prompt for eliciting knowledge. Amongst Spencer Chapman's collection of photographs (held at the Pitt Rivers Museum) are five which have been taken by another unidentified man in Tibet, but which have been used as a cross between a page from *Notes and Queries* (the handbook of British anthropology since the 1870s) and a postcard. They have clearly been sent to Chapman due to his Tibetological expertise to raise questions about the ethnology of the region. One photograph shows a woman standing with a large wooden cylinder. A handwritten message on the reverse asks 'Is this woman making tea – if so, how do they do it?' Another depicts yak herdsmen lunching outside a rest house in Dochen (south of Lhasa) and enquires if the meat they are eating is dried by the wind and sun 'somewhat similar to the North American Indian's Pemmican?' This comparison suggests that the author is an amateur anthropologist with some awareness of Native American cultural practices and someone who recognises the limitations of the photographic record when it is not supplemented by knowledge of indigenous practices. Such photographic exchanges also reiterate the sense in which photography trumpeted the achievements of its producers in having access to first-hand 'authentic knowledge'. The photograph becomes a badge of honour, like a long service medal for those who have fought on the frontline of British incursions into new territories.

An exchange of images also provides a vignette to summarise some of the issues raised in this essay. When Gould introduced the celebration of Christmas into Lhasa at a party for aristocrats' children in 1936 (with the Mission interpreter Norbhu disguised as Father Christmas and a tree decorated with English toys), it was

Woman Making Tea
Unknown Photographer

A woman making tea at Dochen, her face smeared with caoutchoc *(a product of gum elastic) as protection against the sun. The caption on reverse reads: '...butter, soda etc. all together and then add the hot water or do they add cold water and bring the whole to the boil. Why do Tibetan women smear their faces with this red substance, like sealing wax. Is it because of the cold wind?'*
PRM 1998.131.169.

DOCHEN.
Is this woman making tea, if so how do they do it; do they pound the tea, butter, soda etc. all together and then add hot water or do they add cold water and bring the whole to the boil.
Why do Tibetan women smear their faces with this red substance, like sealing wax, is it because of the cold winds?

Men Eating Meat
Unknown Photographer

Yak herdsmen outside the rest house at Dochen eating dried meat. The meat – sha kampo *– is usually smoked, rather than dried in the sun. The grazing is very good around Dochen, and most houses have a special room for storing meat which is cut into strips and hung up to dry. The caption on the reverse reads: '...dried meat, that is, dried by the wind and sun somewhat similar to the North American Indian's Pemmican?'*
PRM 1998.131.168.

another diplomatic tactic designed to provide justification for perpetuating the Mission. Gould insisted that he could not leave Lhasa before the highpoint of the Christian year and in a spirit of rather disingenuous equanimity suggested that he must also stay for Tibetan New Year, which according to the Tibetan calendar was conveniently later than January. He claimed it would have been a discourtesy to leave before the Tibetan festival – which in 1937 was in February. He also commissioned a Christmas card to be sent to his Tibetan hosts and back to London, appropriately stamped with the Lhasa postmark as testament to the ongoing presence of the Mission in Tibet. Gould's Tibetan Christmas card was once again inspired by a precursor, as Charles Bell had sent a photograph of the Potala to his bosses in London at Christmas,[75] but his innovation was to have the Dalai Lama's palace, the key motif of all Lhasa iconography, painted on his cards by Tibetan artists and in Tibetan style. This appropriation of an indigenous aesthetic should be read as part of Gould's commitment

Potala Palace Christmas Card
Made by Tibetan artists for Basil Gould, 1936

The Potala Palace painted in Tibetan style on daphne bark paper. Sir Basil Gould sent these cards made in Lhasa to friends and colleagues in Tibet and Britain. In 1936 Gould instructed that a Christmas party should be held for Tibetan children at the Dekyi Lingka. The Mission house was decorated with a Christmas tree and Norbhu Dhondhup was disguised as Father Christmas. The party was a great success and the children reportedly requested that Christmas would become an annual event in Lhasa.
PRM 2001.35.394.

Tibetan Artists at Work
Evan Nepean, 1936
A group of Tibetan artists seated on the floor painting Christmas cards for the 1936 Gould Mission.
PRM 2001.35.299.1.

14th Dalai Lama's Family at a Party
Amaury de Riencourt (?), *c.* 1940 ?

Gould describes holding a children's party at the Dekyi Lingka which the Dalai Lama's brothers and sisters attended. He notes that the Dalai Lama was obviously not permitted to attend and so his family collected toys to take back for him.
PRM 1998.131.628.

Ringang's Children at a Party
(opposite)
Frederick Spencer Chapman, 1936–1937

The members of the Mission seemed to be incredibly fond of Tibetan children, describing them as obedient, lively and intelligent. On Gould's birthday and at Christmas they held a children's party at which they would show films, give out toys and play games. Ringang was the official interpreter for the Tibetan Cabinet, educated at Rugby and responsible for installing electricity in Lhasa.
PRM 1998.131.500.

to the promotion of Tibetan cultural uniqueness amongst his contacts back in Britain and as an affirmation of his patronage for all things Tibetan for the Lhasa recipients of the card. For most Tibetans, Christmas was a new game whose rules they were ignorant of, but Dasang Damdul Tsarong had a long-term attachment to the British, instigated when he befriended Sir Charles Bell in the 1920s. Although he did not speak English fluently, one of his four wives, Rinchen Dolma (also known as Mary) had been educated in British India and helped him to communicate with members of the Mission.[76] Born into a peasant family, Tsarong had married into the Tibetan aristocracy and therefore had the resources to host numerous parties at his Lhasa mansion. He also attended many others at the British Mission house where, on one occasion, he became so drunk that he collapsed in the arms of Basil Gould murmuring 'Great Minister, I love you, I love you.'[77] Tsarong had developed a passion for all things novel, modern and British – including photography. It seems that he was also uniquely aware of the tight codes of reciprocation that Christmas implied, and so, having received a copy of Gould's Christmas card (and possibly one of Bell's in 1921), he produced his own

Dasang Damdul Tsarong and His Wife Pema Dolkar
Frederick Spencer Chapman, 1937

Tsarong and Pema Dolkar in New Year dress during celebrations at their home in Lhasa in 1937. This photograph was taken during a party to which Spencer Chapman and other members of the 1936 Mission were invited. Tsarong made special arrangements for electric lights to be brought into the house so that Spencer Chapman could take photographs, which normally would not have been possible due to the darkness of most Tibetan interiors. Spencer Chapman noted that, 'On one side of the room was a high throne for Tsarong, and next to it on the left, another, slightly lower, for his wife, and others, lower still, for the three children. Seats for the guests of the house were arranged on the other side of the room. It was all very simple, and the atmosphere, although dignified, was friendly, and emphasised the patriarchal nature of the family. It would be hard to find a people who can keep up their tradition with greater dignity and less self-consciousness than the Tibetans.' (1938:321)
PRM 1998.131.472.

– but celebrating Tibetan New Year instead. The card was made from a piece of high-quality daphne bark paper to which he attached his own small panoramic photograph of the Potala. He then inscribed the card in Tibetan with the message: 'Good wishes for Losar 1937' and his signature. This small object makes a remarkable statement about Tsarong's engagement with the British and demonstrates his ability to use the technology of the colonials. By making it, he indicated that he was able to depict Lhasa as he saw it and that the camera was a tool that could also be wielded effectively by Tibetans as much as by the British. When sending the card to British (and presumably Tibetan) friends and colleagues, Tsarong was creating his own networks of 'distributed personhood' in which objects carry an inalienable essence of the person who made them.[78] This concept implies that as an object (like Tsarong's card) moves through time and space, it transfers a sense of the 'personhood' of the original owner to all those who handle or view it.

This rare thing (displayed for the first time at the Pitt Rivers Museum in the 'Seeing Lhasa' exhibition [see page 61]) captures the way in which the Tibetans and the British became involved in a process of mirroring one another's desires. With the Potala Palace again acting as a shared focal point, both the British and Tibetans used the camera to reflect the key buildings, events and personalities which encompassed the lived experience of Lhasa in the 1930s and 1940s. It seems that both groups also had a sense that they were making history – or at the very least, producing representations of

Lhasa which would fix it in the minds of others for many decades. Dasang Damdul Tsarong was thus one of the first to become aware of the processes through which Tibet was imagined by (particularly British) others. His photographic practice also coincides with the beginning of Tibetan encounters with certain Western-derived models of modernity. Ultimately the new technologies of mass production explored in the 1930s and 1940s in Lhasa (such as photography, film and telegraphy) have become some of the primary vehicles through which Tibetans now engage with the global community. In the contemporary climate in which the current 14th Dalai Lama appears on television all over the world and when feature films such as 'Kundun' reconstruct Tibet prior to the 1950s, the legacy of this period remains powerfully present.[79]

Tsarong was by no means the only Tibetan to own a camera in 1930s Lhasa (the Regent, for example, is said to have become a keen photographer during the course the Gould Mission), but in order to fully explore the concept of 'intercultural mimesis' we would

Cataract Operation
Frederick Spencer Chapman, 1936

Dr. William Morgan performing a cataract operation at the British Mission surgery in the Dekyi Lingka. Thirty three cataract operations were carried out during the 1936–1937 Mission. The majority of patients were elderly monks whose eyesight had deteriorated from years of scanning religious texts. Instead of spectacles, the Gould Mission gave them free operations to improve their vision.
PRM 1998.131.644.

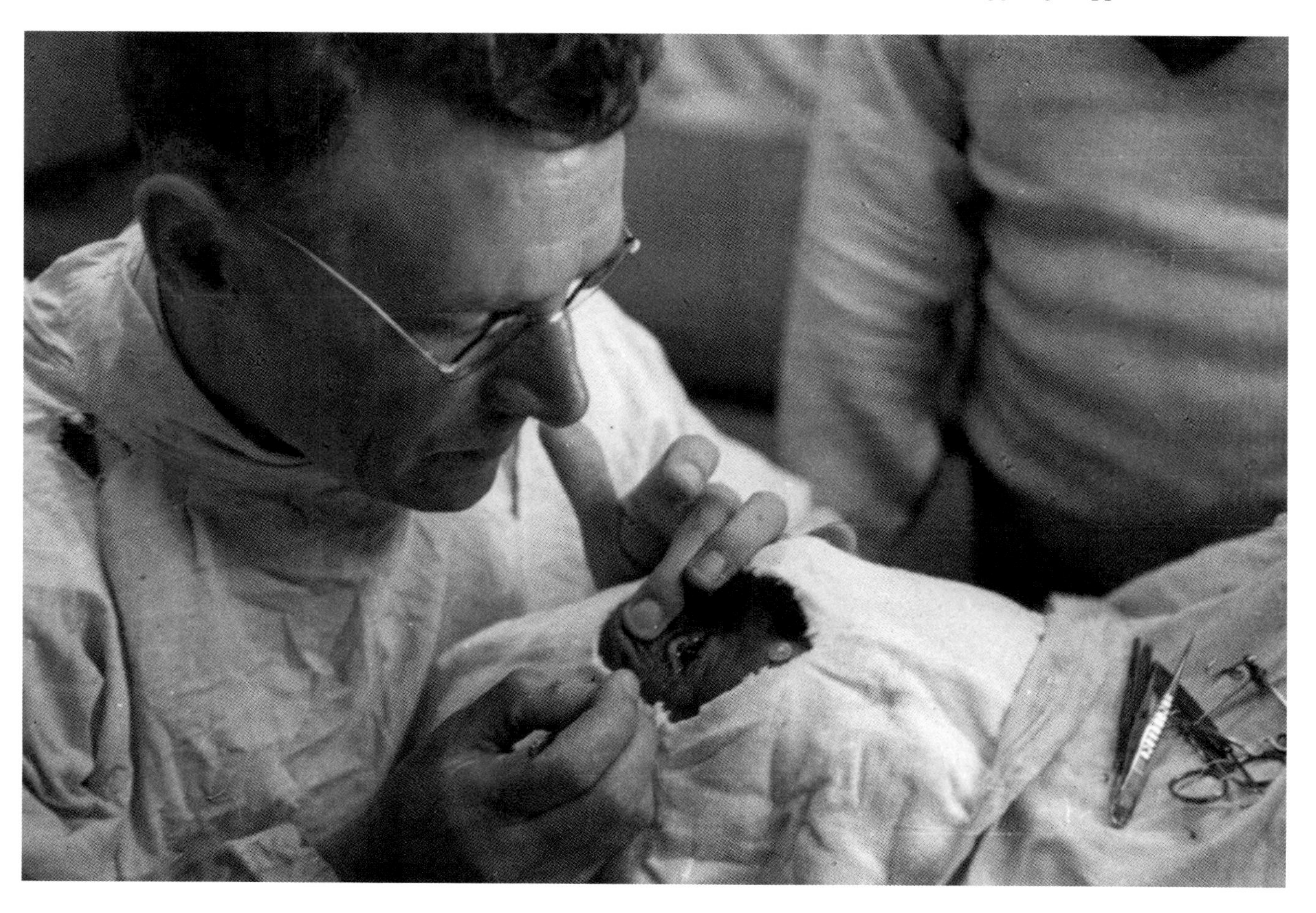

need to consult the photographic archives of Dharamsala and contemporary Lhasa in search of photography made by and for Tibetans.[80] Ideally, this book and exhibition would have treated the visual record of Lhasa with representative images from Tibetan and British sources discussed in equal measure. Since archives of Tibetan photography are only just emerging, we have mainly limited ourselves to British material, concentrating instead on the ways in which the British saw Lhasa at a particular point in time. The period between 1936 and 1947 constitutes a moment when the photographic record achieves a density and complexity that is unusual compared to almost any other time or place in British colonial history. The fact that Tibet lay beyond the well-trodden ground of British India meant that it presented a discreet world which, once penetrated for sufficient time, inspired a concentrated ethnographic and aesthetic engagement on the part of British photographers. The results of this encounter now mean that, like Kipling's monk, we too are presented with an awe-inspiring record of the British vision of Tibet – a record which enables us to continue to see Lhasa as it was before the calamitous events of the 1950s.

Objects in a Lhasa Monastery
Hugh Richardson, *c.* 1936–1950

A Tibetan statue of the great master Padmasambhava (act. in Tibet 8th century) accompanied by a Western-style clock in a glass case.
PRM 2001.59.18.17.1.

Notes

1. Teshoo Lama (a corruption of Tashi Lama) is the term used for the Panchen Lama in many early British publications such as Captain Samuel Turner's 1806 record: 'An Account of an Embassy to the Court of the Teshoo Lama, in Tibet'.
2. Kipling 1901 [1987]:54.
3. Kipling 1901 [1987]:55.
4. Kipling 1901 [1987]:55.
5. Curzon in Anderson 1992:179 n30.
6. Kipling 1901 [1987]:60. Stanley Abe includes a thoughtful discussion of this passage in his essay 'Inside the Wonder House' in Lopez 1995.
7. The 13th Dalai Lama (1876–1933) is said to have instructed that no Tibetan should wear glasses in his presence. However, by the 1930s and 1940s many Tibetans did indulge in their use. See Richardson's portrait of Surkhang, the Minister of Foreign Affairs wearing glasses.
8. The gifts chosen for the new Dalai Lama are interesting in themselves as ambassadorial representatives of British material culture. Gould presented: 'a brick of gold, fresh from the Calcutta Mint, ten sacks of silver, three rifles, six rolls of broadcloth of different colours, a gold watch and chain, field glasses, an English saddle, a picnic case, three stoves, a musical box and a garden hammock.' Gould 1957:227 On an earlier occasion Gould had presented – 'a gold clock with a nightingale that pops out and sings, a pedal motor-car and a tricycle' Gould 1957:219.
9. Gould: 'No European, so far as I am aware has ever been present in Lhasa at the time of the Installation of a Dalai Lama.' 1957: 209 However, other members of his mission, such as the medic Harry Staunton, were also in Lhasa at the time. He made a film during this visit (held at PRM) and may have been responsible for filming the installation ceremony. (See Gould archive at the British Film Insititute.) Amongst Tibetans, Jigme Taring is said to have filmed the occasion.
10. Nor do we intend to produce a comprehensive survey of all British photography of this period. Instead, the exhibition and this essay concentrate on material now held in the Pitt Rivers Museum, which proffers a high density of images and a very particular contextual setting within the University of Oxford, one of the key institutions in which colonial cadres were educated in the United Kingdom. We are aware that German, Austrian, Japanese, French, Italian and American photographers also visited Tibet at this time, but the cultural politics of their engagement with Tibet is likely to reflect quite different agendas which are beyond the scope of our project.
11. See Bishop 1989, Brauen 2000, Lopez 1998, Dodin and Räther 2001.
12. An important exception is Peter Hansen (1995, 1996), whose work on Tibetan film and public spectacle has raised the crucial issues of the relationship between colonial power and the cultural institutions through which this power is mediated.
13. Gell 1999
14. See Appadurai 1986, Hoskins 1998, Thomas 1991, MacKenzie 1991.
15. See Edwards 2001, Poole 1997, Nordstrom 1995.
16. For a lengthier discussion of this topic see Harris 1999.
17. The process of ethnologising subjects of the British Empire was well under way in mid-nineteenth century in India. By the 1880s, L.A. Waddell was using a camera to document Tibetan 'types' which he published in *Among the Himalayas*, his account of life in Darjeeling. See my discussion in Harris 1999.
18. Hallisey 1995:33.
19. In arguing for a repositioning of the relationship between informants and anthropologists, James Clifford's 1997 essay 'Travelling Cultures' acknowledges the interdependency of such relationships historically and the need to move away from such imbalanced power structures in the present.
20. See Gombrich 2000.
21. Thomas Paar also had a studio in Darjeeling where Tibetans were photographed. Images produced in both studios are now held in many museum collections.
22. See Tagg 1988.

23. Abe 1995:96
24. Sadly, Waddell's original photographs have yet to come to light in any private or museum collection.
25. As Michael Aris notes, Bell's successors Hugh Richardson and Basil Gould also took 'Greats' at Oxford. (See Aris in McKay 1997:viii) British colonial officers were often indebted to one another's scholarship and an epistemological lineage was established dating back to Waddell. His *Lhasa and its Mysteries* appears as a source for Spencer Chapman's *Lhasa; The Holy City.* Sir Charles Bell wrote the introduction for it and in turn, Spencer Chapman acknowledges Bell's publications such as *The People of Tibet, Tibet Past and Present* and *The Religion of Tibet.* The same works are cited by Gould in his autobiography *The Jewel in the Lotus.* Hence, though some senior political officers such as Richardson, Bell and Gould learnt Tibetan (Gould published books on Tibetan language accompanied by gramophone recordings of song) – the primary source of information on Tibet were these English language publications. For more information on Bell see biographical entry in this volume.
26. For an account of Bell's relationship with the 13th Dalai Lama see Bell's 1946 publication *Portrait of a Dalai Lama.* The majority of Bell's glass plate negatives are now housed at the Pitt Rivers Museum, Oxford. Prints are held at the Liverpool Museum and the British Library.
27. Goldstein 1982:56.
28. Richardson was resident in Lhasa representing the British Government from 1936–1940 and working for the Indian Government from 1947–1950. See biographical entry in this volume. Unfortunately we have not had access to the Richardson papers deposited at the Bodleian Library (Oxford) in 2001 as their release was intended to coincide with the Tenth Seminar of the IATS (September 2003).
29. For further information on the importance of the Dekyi Lingka see the essay by Tsering Shayka in this volume.
30. McKay 2001:78. Bell also arranged for four Tibetan boys to be educated at a famous English public school, Rugby. On their return to Tibet they performed important liaison duties between the British and the Tibetans. One of them, Ringang, was also responsible for engineering the electrification of Lhasa using machinery acquired in England in 1924.
31. McKay 2001:85.
32. Frederick Spencer Chapman, Private Secretary to Gould deciphered telegrams, kept a metrological log, collected and pressed flowers (for Kew), dried seeds, made notes on bird life and kept the official Diary of the Mission which was sent back to London each week (accompanied by photographs). See biographical entry in this volume.
33. Landon 1905:157.
34. Bishop 1994:6.
35. Abe 1995:67.
36. However, these images were for private albums and not included in any publication.
37. See the photographers' biographical entries at the end of this volume.
38. Gould 1957:204.
39. The tendency to feminise Lhasa and/or the Potala is also evident in Waddell's account of his visit to the city in 1904: 'Wreathed in the romance of centuries, Lhasa, the secret citadel of the 'undying' Grand Lama, has stood shrouded in impenetrable mystery on the Roof-of-the-World, alluring yet defying our most adventurous travellers to enter her closed gates ... But now, in the fateful Tibetan Year of the Wood Dragon, the fairy Prince of Civilisation has roused her from her slumbers, her closed doors are broken down, her dark veil of mystery is lifted up and the long sealed shrine with its grotesque cults and its idolised Grand Lama, shorn of his sham nimbus, have yielded up their secrets and lie disenchanted before our Western eyes.' (*Lhasa and its Mysteries*) See Harris 1999 for further discussion.
40. As recorded by the Tibetan finance minister and historian Shakabpa quoted in Douglas (2001).
41. *Mission Diary,* August 31s, 'This was the first perfectly clear sunny morning we have had, with not a cloud in the sky at sunrise, a perfect morning for photographing the imposing and beautiful south face of the Potala.'

42. Mountaineering was an important activity for the British in the Himalayas and the attempt to scale Everest took up much diplomatic time. See Hansen 1996.
43. For a wider discussion of British colonial photography and landscape aesthetics see Ryan 1997.
44. *Mission Diary* 3rd September 'The Tsuglakhang (JoKhang) it is in the centre of the city and one nowhere gets a proper view of it. From a neighbouring rooftop we took photos of its golden roofs.'
45. The positioning of such vantage points was selected with care as Tibetan protocol dictated that if the Dalai Lama or a similarly high-ranking figure were passing by in procession nobody should be able to look down on him. An interesting comparison can be drawn between British photographs of Lhasa processions and those taken in the 1940s by Dundul Namgyal Tsarong – who clearly took his pictures of the same ceremonies from street level. See D. N. Tsarong, *Tibet as it Was*, 1990.
46. Spencer Chapman's 1936 use of Kodachrome 16 mm film in Tibet marks him out as a pioneer in the history of filmmaking. It was only in 1935 that Dufaycolour had been used for the first time to film King George V's Silver Jubilee in London and 150 copies of the film were distributed to cinema halls for public viewing. The use of this new and expensive technology in Tibet was typical of Spencer Chapman's adventurous nature and testimony to Basil Gould's sense of the importance of his Mission. An edited version of his film made in Tibet (1936–1937) and that of Harry Staunton (1940) was produced for the exhibition 'Seeing Lhasa'.
47. Spencer Chapman 1938:262
48. See McKay 2001
49. Spencer Chapman 1937:122.
50. Gould's immediate predecessor, Frederick Williamson, produced a good number of photographs during his stint as Political Officer for Sikkim, Bhutan and Tibet. He made two visits to Lhasa and the photographic record of these missions are preserved in albums at the Cambridge University Museum of Archaeology and Anthropology.
51. 'Colour film of Tibet, Mr B J Gould's journey', *Times*, 20 July 1937
52. Spencer Chapman 1937:125.
53. Hansen 2001:97.
54. 'We had a special arrangement with Kodak in London. As soon as he (Spencer Chapman) had taken a few rolls of 'Kodachrome' film they were sent off by Tibetan post to Gyantse, which took about four days, then by the Trade Agent's post to Gangtok which took another two or three days; and from India by air to London. Kodak gave them priority and telegraphed out comments. In a little more than month the films would be back in Lhasa, to the delight of all who came to see them.' Gould 1957: 206.
55. Spencer Chapman 1938:246.
56. Spencer Chapman 1938:246.
57. Draft versions of these albums assembled in Lhasa in 1936 have been loaned to the Pitt Rivers Museum for the exhibition, 'Seeing Lhasa'.
58. R. Peel to Gould 30 Aug 1944 L/P&S/12/4180 OIOC cited in Hansen 2001:103.
59. Gould to E. P. Donaldson, undated February 1946, 'one of our main political aims [was]showing that Tibet had its own art etc and that in some ways Tibet is more closely allied to India than to China.' Quoted in McKay 2001:78
60. Reting Rinpoche was meant to serve as Regent until the new (14th) Dalai Lama reached his majority (typically at age 21). However, he stepped down in 1941 amid rumours that he was unfit for office. See Tsering Shakya's essay in this volume for further discussion and Goldstein (1989) for a full account of his regency between 1934 and 1941.
61. *Mission Diary*, Friday, 28th August, 'Neame and Chapman were allowed to take photos of the Regent; amongst his attendants was a giant lama, some 7-feet high, and when Neame snapped him he began to talk and wave his arms. These were not threatening gestures as he was only asking for a copy of the photo.'
62. *Mission Diary*, 21st September.
63. Exceptionally, Lady Lhalu, Mary Taring and the Tsarong wives were present at many gatherings. At least three British men married Tibetan women – George Bogle (in

Lascham Lhalu
Hugh Richardson, *c.* 1936–1950

Portrait of Lascham (Lady) Lhalu in a garden. Gould notes that she was 'A member of high society … connected by birth with the two previous Dalai Lamas, [and] who lived on her estate a mile off. In 1904 it had been the headquarters of the Younghusband Expedition to Lhasa. One of the events of the Lhasa season was an annual luncheon party which she gave to the Cabinet and other high officials. Her hospitality was so urgent that often the fate of at least a few of her guests was "Where I dines I sleeps". She had a fund of jokes and stories which were reputed to be broad. I doubt whether even in England men and women live on such natural and easy terms as in Tibet.' (1957:236)
PRM 2001.59.7.2.1.

the 18th century), Henry Martin in the 1910s and Reggie Fox, the wireless operator in Lhasa in the 1940s.

64. Spencer Chapman wrote: 'At first they were a little suspicious, especially the poorer people, and more particularly of the big cinema camera which made a formidable noise and, with its long telephoto lens, resembled some new-fangled automatic gun.' (1938:247)
65. See McKay 2001 and 1994
66. Williamson 1987:206
67. Hansen (1996) discusses the film of the ascent of Everest shown in London and reported in the British papers. When Tibetans heard that the film included scenes of their countrymen apparently eating lice from one another's bodies, they were outraged.
68. 'The sight of themselves on film was convincing proof to Tibetan audiences that what they saw was real.' Gould 1957:206.
69. Gould 1957:207.
70. For an important discussion of the formats in which photographs circulate see Edwards, E. in Kwint, Breward and Aynsley (Eds) 1999
71. For analysis of Tibetan photo-icons and their circulation see Harris 1999 and 2001.
72. Therefore, in the 19th century, Waddell's collection of Tibetan material had been sent to the British Museum. See Harris 1999 and for wider analysis of such projects see Richards 1993.
73. Richardson's copy is now held in the British Museum
74. Though the Pitt Rivers Museum (PRM) has much of the material to do this, we do not have access to the photographic collections of key figures such as Colonel Neame, who was a major contributor to the 1936 photographic project.
75. A copy of Bell's Christmas card (incorporating a photograph of the Potala) from Lhasa is held in the Liverpool Museum.
76. See Rinchen Dolma (Mary) Taring's *Daughter of Tibet* on her work for her first husband Tsarong's business which involved translating letters into English.
77. Gould 1957:236.
78. See Gell (1998) on the concept of distributed personhood and Harris (2001) for a discussion of this topic relating it to the use of Dalai Lama photo-icons
79. On complicity with outsider representations in contemporary Tibetan communities see Harris (1999) and Lopez (1998).
80. In recent years a number of photographic archives have been established in the Tibetan exile community in Dharamsala (India) at the Tibet Museum and Visual Archive, the Amnye Machen Institute and Department of International Relations. Publications on photography by Tibetans are scant but include Dundul Namgyal Tsarong's *What Tibet Was* (which features his own photographs and some taken by his father Dasang Damdul Tsarong) and a special issue of the Taiwanese journal *Photographers International* which is dedicated to the Tibetan photographer Lobsang Demo (1901–1973).

Entrance to the Tsuglakhang

Frederick Spencer Chapman, 1936–1937

The 7th century Tsuglakhang (Jo khang) is the spiritual centre of Tibet and an important pilgrimage site due to the presence of the Jo Shakyamuni (an image of the Buddha as a child). In this image we also see evidence of the modernisation of Lhasa in the form of street lamps.
PRM 1998.131.347.

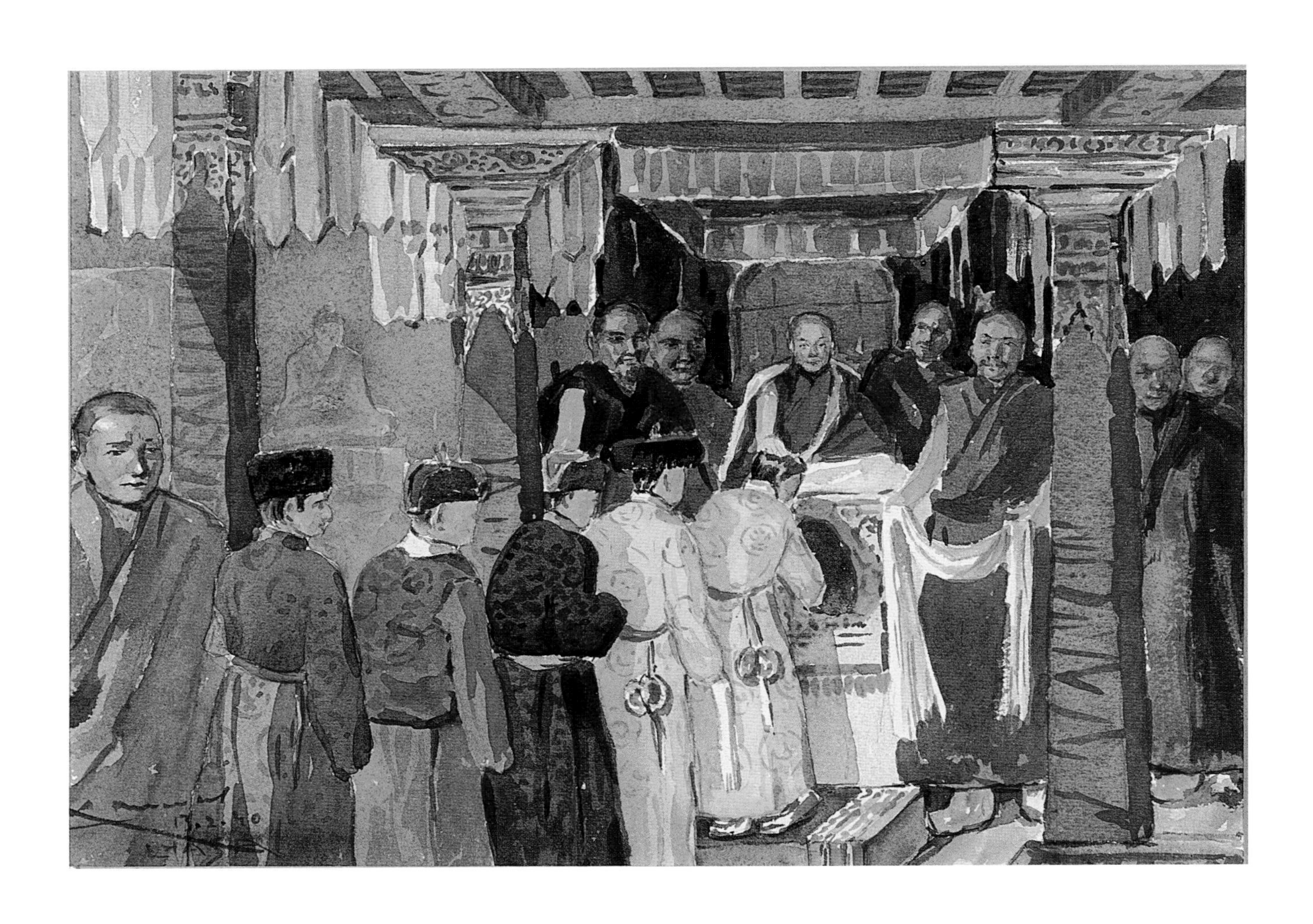

Cities and Thrones and Powers: The British and the Tibetans in Lhasa, 1936–1947

Tsering Shakya

Lhasa Remembered

As a child, we were repeatedly told how fortunate we were to be born in Lhasa. This was the truth as told by the elders and we were happy to accept it. After all, we knew nothing else. The outside world simply did not exist, even in our wildest imaginings. Lhasa was not only the place of our dreams but a place where we lived. We heard the tales of how the Tsuglakhang (or Jo khang) was built on a lake. During the day the mortals laboured and at night, when man slept, the angels descended to the earth and assisted in the building. In the inner circumambulation route of the temple, you can stroll around the dimly lit cobble-stoned passages where there is a concave stone. We were told that if we bent low and pressed an ear closely to it, we would hear the water churning underground. When I did this, I heard a sort of swishing sound and knew that what I had been told was the truth.

Growing up in Lhasa in the1960s was a strange affair – it was the beginning of my life but it was the end of Tibet. When I was only five or six years old, my mother and some of her friends took me and some other children to the site near Drepung monastery where corpses are dismembered. There a large flat stone slab was used as a table to cut up the corpses, which were then fed to the vultures. I was made to roll on the large stone slab back and forth several times. My mother explained that by doing this, I would lose all fear of death. She said that one day everyone must face death and that my body too would

The Installation of the 14th Dalai Lama (opposite)
Kanwal Krishna, 1940

Tibetan dignitaries waiting to present katak *(silk scarves) to the 14th Dalai Lama at his Installation ceremony in the Potala Palace.*
Private Collection.

The Peacock Tent
Hugh Richardson, 1939

The Peacock tent, decorated with silk fabrics for the arrival of the 14th Dalai Lama in Lhasa in 1939 at the age of four and a half, following his recognition in Amdo (northeastern Tibet). A party travelled to the outskirts of Lhasa to greet the new incarnation, including the British Representative in Lhasa, Hugh Richardson. Richardson was therefore the first foreign national to meet the young Dalai Lama and he wrote that: 'he Dalai Lama was … led to a throne inside a gaily coloured reception tent, hung with golden brocade.' (1998:673) In this image, Norbhu Dondhup stands next to the throne.
PRM 2001.59.18.9.1.

be cut and tossed to the vultures. It wasn't just the children who did this; even adults would roll on the slabs whenever they had a chance to pass by. I don't know why mother took me that particular day – perhaps she feared that death might come soon. And I still don't know whether this is a old Tibetan custom, or something that developed in response to a particularly bleak situation. But such things stay in one's memory. My childhood memory of Lhasa is full of similar seemingly disconnected events.

In 1996 when I visited Lhasa for the first time since leaving Tibet in 1967, I went to the Tsuglakhang as all Tibetans do. I tried to locate the exact spot where we used to press our ears closely to the sacred ground. While I found the dented cobblestone, it seems that the practice has disappeared. Nor, did I see anyone rolling over the stone slab on which the corpses are dismembered. Like much of Lhasa, the customs I remember from my childhood have disappeared and only linger in the mind's eye. Like many of us visiting childhood places, we tend to search for the landmarks of memory, the house where we lived and places we frequented. For me, one of those places is the Dekyi Lingka, former residence and office of the British Mission in Lhasa. This modest Tibetan house represented the prestige of the British Empire to Tibetans – what the colonial mandarins liked to call 'showing the flag'. It seemed at the time, that the Union Jack fluttered over the Dekyi Lingka ever since the Christian god breathed life into an English man. But the reality is that the British Mission in Lhasa was only established in August 1936 and came to an

The Dekyi Lingka (opposite)
Frederick Spencer Chapman, 1936–1937

The Dekyi Lingka ('Garden of Happiness'), home to the British in Lhasa for several decades, with Union Jack flying and 1936 Mission members Evan Nepean and William Morgan on the balcony. According to Spencer Chapman the living arrangements were as follows: 'We found the actual house somewhat small for our requirements. Gould and Neame occupied two minute rooms upstairs; the doctor took possession of an even smaller ground-floor room opening off the tiny kitchen courtyard, while Richardson and I put up our tents in the walled garden. There was one rather gloomy downstairs room which we used as a dining-room, and a more cheerful one above with a verandah that we roofed in with canvas and used for receptions. Neame's bedroom afterwards became Gould's office, while the five Sikkimese clerks had a large office a hundred yards from our house. The kitchens and stables were part of the main building. Norbhu found quarters just outside our main doorway between the kitchen and the stables.' (1938:229–230)
PRM 1998.131.376.

The Garden at the Dekyi Lingka
Hugh Richardson, *c.* 1936–1950

The Dekyi Lingka garden teemed with insects and birds (a boon for the ornithologists on the Mission) and groves of trees were much appreciated for screening out the dust of the city. The English-style planting reminded many British visitors of home. In 1944, the Dekyi Lingka gardens were expanded by Sherriff and Ludlow.
PRM 2001.59.18.4.1.

Nepean's Tent at the Dekyi Lingka
Evan Nepean, 1936

Evan Nepean's tent in the garden of the Dekyi Lingka (the British Mission house). Evan Nepean and Sidney Dagg were responsible for the telegraph equipment brought to Lhasa by the British in 1936. Since there was no electricity supply to the Dekyi Lingka, they charged up their generators in the houses of Tibetan friends (such as Ringang). Along with carrying out his official duties of communication, Nepean contacted a number of amateur enthusiasts around the world with his call signal AC4YN. Before this, the only telegraph machine in Lhasa was owned by the Chinese and so the presence of the British equipment undermined their monopoly on the flow of information in and out of the city.
PRM 2001.35.375.

end on 15 August 1947. Longevity is not the sole criterion to judge the importance of such institutions, and the aura of power and authority that manifested in this small building ensures that its reputation and fame remains. For a decade, the Dekyi Lingka was a little England on the arid Tibetan plateau. Even the name has an English lilt, meaning as it does 'Happy Garden', which is like so many other places in the Empire named by the British, such as 'Happy Valley' or 'Rose Cottage'. Perhaps it was the name that first drew the British to this house in the outskirts of Lhasa. When accompanying Younghusband into Lhasa on 3 August 1904, Edmund Candler, correspondent for the Daily Mail, wrote in his diary, 'Butterflies and dragon-flies were hovering among the rushes, clematis grew in the stoneworks by the roadside, cows were grazing in the rich pastureland, redshanks were calling, a flight of teal passed overhead: *the whole scene was most home like.*'[1] Similarly, Basil Gould much later wrote, 'Tibetans laugh at just the same things and in the same tone, and appreciated beauty in just the same things, as Englishmen.'[2]

For a decade, this modest house in Lhasa might as well have been the pleasure dome of Kublai Khan. The Dekyi Lingka came to be associated with glamour and the marvel of the world outside. Those few powerful and privileged Tibetans who had the chance to be entertained at the lavish parties hosted by the head of the Mission could enjoy the latest fads, technology and fashion from the world beyond the snow peaks. As we can see from the collection of photographs in this volume, the British representatives documented the lives

Dr. Morgan's Surgery in Lhasa
Frederick Spencer Chapman, 1936–1937

Dr William Morgan (right) and two orderlies inoculating a young woman against venereal disease. It was part of the British policy to give free medical attention to Tibetans in Lhasa. The 'surgery' was in an out-building at the Dekyi Lingka. Venereal disease was rife in Lhasa in the 1930s and 40s. Those high enough in rank could get private house calls from Morgan to avoid the embarrassment of showing up at the open-plan surgery. Hence, Morgan probably knew far more about the personal lives of many Tibetans than other members of the Mission. The British medical presence in Lhasa was formalised in 1940 with the building of a hospital under the supervision of Dr. Harry Staunton.
PRM 1998.131.398.

Kundeling Dzasa (Temba Wangchuk)
Frederick Spencer Chapman, 1936–1937

The Kundeling Dzasa took care of the estates of Kundeling monastery and was a leading power in the National Assembly. He was also the landlord for the 1936 Mission as Kundeling monastery owned the Dekyi Lingka. He is described by Spencer Chapman as a man of 'great character' with a firm 'but humorous' mouth and bright intelligent eyes. 'Though he has never in his life been more than thirty miles from Lhasa, he showed a lively interest in many subjects. He asked us, for instance, if motor-cars had entirely superseded horses in England as a means of transport; and the relative times it would take to get from Calcutta to London by air, by steamer, and on foot.' (1938:204–205)
PRM 1998.157.33.

of their Tibetans visitors both visually and in extensive documentation. The monthly and weekly reports submitted to the Political Officer in Gangtok in Sikkim, which eventually made their way to the desks of civil servants in Whitehall, recorded meticulously the names of visitors, the type of food served and the type of entertainment provided. These gatherings provided an opportunity for the British to gather the latest gossip about who was in favour and who was in and out of Lhasa politics. Kundeling Dzasa, who had built the Dekyi Lingka as a *tro ti khang* (pleasure house) – a sort of English country house, threatened to evict the British from from time to time – perhaps in the hopes of extracting a higher rent. Therefore, like all good tenants, the diplomatic British did their best to ingratiate themselves with Kundeling in order to maintain harmonious relations.

My own connection to the Dekyi Lingka happened by accident, a chance only created by a major calamity – in this case, the Sino-Indian border war. In 1962, the impact of the war began to be felt in Lhasa, remote as it was and shielded by the most formidable mountain range in the world. The British had left the Dekyi Lingka in 1947, when India gained her independence, and it had subsequently become the Indian Mission in Lhasa. As the tension between India and China grew, the Indian Mission was expelled. I do not know the reasons, but my eldest brother – who worked at the time as a translator for the Nepalese Consulate in Lhasa – was sent to look after the building with his family. My mother, aware of the tension in the city as a result of the Sino-Indian conflict, felt that the Dekyi Lingka would be a safe refuge, so I was sent to live there with my brother until I was about seven. By the Tibetan standards of the time, the Dekyi Lingka was like a palace, far more luxurious than most homes in Lhasa. I was too young to know the historical significance of the house, but even a child could see it was different from anything you saw within the city centre.

Later in my life, another connection with the Dekyi Lingka emerged. When I came to England, I went to a boarding school where Dick Gould was serving as headmaster. He was the son of Sir Basil Gould who first acquired the Dekyi Lingka and established it as

Sir Basil Gould meeting the Dalai Lama's Family
Harry Staunton, *c.* 1940

Sir Basil Gould shaking hands with the Dalai Lama's mother. To his right is the Dalai Lama's father and Norbhu Dhondhup. This photograph was probably taken at the time of the Installation of Tenzin Gyatso as the 14th Dalai Lama. His mother, the Gyayum Chenmo ('Great Mother'), was a distinctive figure in Lhasa as she always dressed in the Amdo style (the region of Tibet from which the family came) and wore her hair in three plaits. Gould described her as 'one in a million' and it seems that they were on friendly terms as the 'Great Mother' stayed with the Gould family when she visited Britain in the 1960s.
PRM 1999.23.1.27.3.

the British Mission office. On the walls of Dick's house in Romsey, there hung water-colour portraits of important Tibetan figures. I later discovered they were by the Indian artist Kanwal Krishna, who had travelled with Basil Gould to Lhasa in 1940, when the latter had been invited to the Installation ceremony of the 14th Dalai Lama. I was fascinated with the figures in this series of paintings, as they were of Tibetans political and religious figures whose names I had heard many times before.

During its time as the British Mission, an invitation to the Dekyi Lingka signified for a Tibetan recognition of their status and political importance. On the other hand, the British interpreted a visit by a Tibetan official as a favourable inclination towards the British presence. Tenpa Jamyang, the first monk official to be appointed Commander in Chief of the Tibetan army, was noted in the 1934 *Who's Who in Tibet* as, 'not very favourably inclined towards the British but in 1936 came to call on the Political Officer which he had not done in previous Missions.'

'We could run the whole show'[3]

By the 1930s, there was a sizeable number of Tibetan aristocrats who could be called Anglophiles. Educated in schools in England and India, they had become aware of the customs and manners of the colonial officials. Many could converse in English and found that they had much in common with the upper circles of British colonial officials. It was a meeting of taste and manners. The British residents in Lhasa were quick to compare life in Blighty with the situation in Lhasa. In many ways, the social delineation in both societies was broadly similar. The Dalai Lama's family could be compared to the British monarchy, the aristocracy's manners and customs could have easily been accommodated in English society and the church with its ecclesiastical hierarchy and the elaborate rituals resembled high Anglicanism. At the base, there were the workers who toiled the fields. The social hierarchy in Tibet exuded familiarity for the British, and they were quick to find equivalence as a means of comprehending and accommodating their Tibetan counterparts.

The British therefore often transposed Tibetan social ranks to their English equivalent. The title Kung was given to the father or closest relative of the reigning Dalai Lama. Being a direct descendent of 'royal'

Kanwal Krishna painting a Portrait of the Nechung Oracle
Photographer unknown, 1940

The Indian artist Kanwal Krishna making a portrait of the State Oracle in his throne room at Nechung monastery. The watercolour is reproduced on page 115.
Courtesy of Chitrangada Sharma.

Yabzhi Phünkang (Tashi Dorje) Kung
Frederick Spencer Chapman, 1936–1937

The Yabzhi Phünkang Kung (known to the British as 'The Duke') was a member of the Lhasa aristocracy and later became a Shapé in the Tibetan Cabinet (Kashag). The title of Kung (or 'Duke') is originally conferred on the father or brother of the reigning Dalai Lama. In this case, Phünkang was the name of the family of the 11th Dalai Lama [1838–1856]). Spencer Chapman describes the subject of this portrait as, 'The Duke ... a tall lean man with such bad sight that he has to hold everything up to his eyes before he can see it. He gives the impression of being completely absent-minded and unpractical in a very aristocratic and charming way.' (1938:79)
PRM 1998.131.625.

blood, the title was translated as 'Duke'. Less formal titles such as Kusho were translated as a 'Sir' or 'Esquire'. When there were no obvious equivalences, the British could call upon the resources of colonial terminology, the Dzongpön became the District Magistrate, Latsemp-pa became *Chaprasi*, an Anglo-Indian term for a clerk. Some terms vexed even the most scholarly-minded colonial officers. One of them 'Dzasa' had the following note affixed in the British Mission files: 'A high title. No English equivalent. Sometimes incorrectly translated as a "Earl", but it is not hereditary.'[4]

One of the duties of the British Mission was to maintain a close watch on the daily political and social affairs of Tibet. The head of the Mission was 'our man on the spot'. The Mission's staff had to compile a list of the leading figures of Tibetan politics, which was later published for internal government circulation as *Who's Who in Tibet*.[5] Today, the document makes interesting reading and shows the British view on the minutiae of Tibetan life.

The biographical notes on Tibetan officials were distilled from observing and talking with the visitors to the Dekyi Lingka, in addition to gossip from the streets of Lhasa, and in summation assessments of the particular subject's stand on Britain were made. This was not an easy task. The *Who's Who* noted that many officials were simply referred to by their titles and for many, it was 'impossible to ascertain their personal names'. To rank them in importance, a star rating was established with three stars indicating a person of the 'the most importance'. For example, Chang Ngopa Ringang, one of the brightest of the boys sent in 1913 to England to study at Rugby, was by 1936 given two stars after his name with the following comments, 'pro-British but cautious'. Chensel Lobzang, a senior courtier of the Panchen Lama's estate, was a 'three-starred' official, described as follows: 'an ordinary monk in Tashilhunpo monastery but became the favourite of the Tashi Lama [ie. the Panchen Lama]'. An extra tidbit of gossip was added: 'Is said to keep a Chinese woman'. Dinga Dorje Gyaltsen, a lay official, is described as someone who 'speaks Hindustani quite fluently, a few words of Chinese and a little English... very intelligent, jovial and sociable and promises to be a great man in the country.' Approval is clearly indicated in the closing sentence of Dinga's record, 'is very pro-British'. Some were not so favourably assessed. The entry for Langcunga Shapé one of the senior members of the Tibetan Cabinet (the Kashag) read: 'very conservative and not very intelligent'. An even more astonishing description in the *Who's Who*

Ringang
Frederick Spencer Chapman,
1936–1937

Ringang (Chang Ngopa Rinzin Dorje, also known as Kusho Chango Pa), a 6th rank official and the official interpreter to the Tibetan Cabinet (Kashag). Ringang was one of the four boys sent to England to be educated at Rugby in 1913 (arranged by Sir Charles Bell and the 13th Dalai Lama). On his return from England he was responsible for installing electricity in Lhasa.
PRM 1998.131.498.

Dinga Dorje Gyaltsen
Kanwal Krishna, 1940

Dinga Dorje Gyaltsen (1896-1945) was sent to Quetta and Shillong in India in 1923 for military training with the British Indian army. While in India he cut his hair short in British army fashion because of the heat and the need to fit in with the British officers. On his return to Tibet in 1924, and under Dasang Damdul Tsarong's direction, he encouraged the other Tibetan officers to wear Western-style uniforms and keep their hair short. However, traditionally aristocrats recruited to serve as lay officials in the government (the drung kor*), had to wear their hair in a top knot known as a* pa chok, *which had a turquoise ornament attached at the top of the crown. When Dinga and other young officers discarded this tradition, there was a certain amount of public criticism. Fearful of the growing power of the army, Tsarong's opponents (particularly the monasteries) took advantage of this criticism and his temporary absence in India, and had all the officers who had cut their hair removed. In 1924, Dinga was relieved from duty until he had grown his hair back and wore it in the traditional style. By the time of this painting in 1940, Dinga was the Dzongpön (District Magistrate) of Shigatse. In 1936, he had headed the welcoming committee for Basil Gould and the British delegation at Gyantse, before escorting them to Lhasa.*
Private Collection.

is that of Trimon Shapé, marked with three stars: 'has suffered from occasional fits of insanity'.

The closeness between the British and Tibetans was the culmination of two centuries of well-planned British engagement with Tibet. However, it was only during the last decade of the British Empire that the policy of wooing the Tibetans and keeping every other foreign power from gaining a foothold on the Tibetan plateau could be fully realised. By the 1930s, the British, who had since the 18th century

Norbhu, Trimon and Tsarong
Frederick Spencer Chapman,
1936–1937

From left to right: Norbhu Dhondhup, Trimon Shapé and Dasang Damdul Tsarong drinking at the Dekyi Lingka. Spencer Chapman describes Trimon thus: 'Trimon, an ex-Shappe, came to call. He is grey-haired and looks old and worried. He has just married a new and attractive wife, in whose Lhasa house he now lives; but soon he returns to Gyantse to occupy some estates he has gained possession of after a long and expensive lawsuit. They say that when he wanted to retire from his duties as a Cabinet minister his resignation was refused by the Dalai Lama, so he took off all his clothes and, feigning madness, ran naked through the streets of Lhasa. He is anything but insane now, though he seems saturnine and disillusioned.' (1938:87)
PRM 1998.131.412.

harboured a desire to establish a permanent office in Lhasa, were justified in being smug about their diplomatic achievements in Tibet. In 1904, Colonel Francis Younghusband, commander of the British invading force, had written to his wife that if the British could establish a office in Lhasa, 'we could run the whole show'.[6] With the British investiture in the Dekyi Lingka, this is the exactly how the Chinese and other foreign powers also perceived the situation. In reality, however, the British position in Lhasa was always precarious, and depended on meeting the Tibetans' chief objective of keeping China out of Tibet. The presence of the British was for the Tibetans a means of demonstrating their independence and the distance from China.

The British policy towards Tibet since the 19th century could be summed up as keeping the Tibetan plateau free of foreign powers. Stretching from the west in Kashmir to the border of Burma in the east, the Himalayas are the natural frontier between British India and Tibet. In the north, the barren Jangthang landscape is a hostile territory for any army and the vast stretch of mountainous landscape in the east was similarly formidable. Thus, Tibet's natural environment provided the British with a safe buffer zone, and the British objective was to keep the Empire safe. Nearly a century of carefully-crafted policy

The Yuthok Sampa (Turquoise Bridge) on the Outskirts of Lhasa
Frederick Spencer Chapman, 1936–1937

Pack mules passing through the Yuthok Sampa (Turquoise Bridge), so-named because of the turquoise-glazed tiles on its roof. Its original construction dates back to the 7th century but it is now used as a billiard hall and tea shop. The Potala Palace is visible beyond.
PRM 1998.131.271.

materialised in the establishment of a permanent British Mission in Lhasa in August 1936.

This was not the first time the British had established a base inside Tibet; since Younghusband's 1904 expedition, the British had maintained trade agent offices in Gyantse, Dromo (Yatung) and in Gartok in Western Tibet. Their primary role was to oversee the Indo-Tibetan trade across the Himalayas, but the British officers who served in these posts were more than tax collectors. Their unique access to the country made them experts in their field and many formed a lifelong obsession with Tibet. Younghusband, for example, was transformed by his encounter with Tibet. About to leave Lhasa, he wandered off alone to the nearby mountains and experienced something that could only be described as a spiritual epiphany. He wrote later:

> *I went off alone to the mountain-side and gave myself up to all the emotions of this eventful time. My task was over and every anxiety*

was passed. The scenery was in sympathy with my feelings: the unclouded sky a heavenly blue; the mountain softly merging into violet; and, as I now looked towards that mysterious purply haze in which the sacred city was once more wrapped ... I was insensibly suffused with an almost intoxicating sense of elation and good-will. This exhilaration of the moment grew and grew till it thrilled through me with overpowering intensity. Never again could I think evil, or ever again be at enmity with any man. All nature and all humanity were bathed in a rosy glowing radiancy; and life for the future seemed nought but buoyancy and light ... And that single hour on leaving Lhasa was worth all the rest of a lifetime.[7]

Lhasa: A City of Fortune

For Tibetans, Lhasa represented what Mecca represents for Muslims: the holiest of all religious sites and the centre of the Tibetan cultural world. While Western travellers saw Lhasa as 'the forbidden city', in many ways, it was deeply cosmopolitan, attracting merchants from all over Asia to trade or make their fortunes. In 1722, Ippolito Desideri, a Jesuit missionary arrived in Lhasa and described the city as full of merchants from many places: Tartars, Chinese, Muscovites, Armenians, Kashimiris, Hindustanis and Nepalese.[8] There is evidence that Armenian merchant s were frequent visitors to Lhasa trading in musk and amber. For the Newars of the Kathmandu Valley, Lhasa was a source of wealth; in Lakshimiprasad Devkota's epic poem 'Muna Madan', the main protagonist goes to Lhasa to make his fortune and leaves the city with a purse of gold.

Since the time of Pratap Malla (r. 1637–1671) the rulers of the Kathmandu Valley had had an established office in Lhasa with a military escort of several hundred. In the subsequent Shah dynasty (1768–present), this office was known as the Gorkha Lekung and the head of the office known as the Gorkha Pönpo was a powerful presence in Lhasa long before the British entered the scene. The Nepalese also had an office in Shigatse, and the representative there was called the Shar Pönpo (Eastern Head). From the late 18th century, the Nepalese acquired greater power in Tibet than any other foreign government, and had rights to establish further offices in Phari, Gyantse and Kyirong. It is odd that when writing about the history of Tibet, most writers have highlighted the prominence of China and Britain – but have ignored the strength of the Gorkhas in Tibet.

Ladakhi Muslims in Lhasa
Frederick Spencer Chapman, 1936–1937

In the 1930s, there were around two to three hundred Muslims in Lhasa. When the 5th Dalai Lama (1617–1682) took Ladakh into his sphere of influence after 1642, a small community of Muslims established themselves in Lhasa as traders and butchers. They were known as 'Khache' *(Kashmiri) and had their own mosque in the southeastern corner of the city. In 1936, two of the Ladakhi Muslims (named Gulam Maidin Mahommad and Asatulla Mahommad) visited Sir Basil Gould to ask for extra-territorial rights on the grounds that Ladakh was part of British India. Gould did not consider the Ladakhis to be oppressed in any way and therefore rejected the request. The Ladakhis also created a football team to take on the British in Lhasa, and lost.*
PRM 1998.131.284.

There is an interesting story told of the Gorkhas in Lhasa. Some time during 1920, the 13th Dalai Lama (1876–1933) and his retinue were approaching the Yuthok Sampa, the famed turquoise-tiled bridge outside Lhasa. On the other side the Gorkha Pönpo was approaching on his horse. Whenever the Dalai Lama's party approaches, Tibetan custom requires all other riders to dismount. The Gorkha Pönpo was either unaware that Tibet's highest pontiff was approaching from the other side or he was deliberately asserting the status of his nation. The sight of a haughty figure on a horse incensed a young courtier named Chogyal Nyima whose duty was to walk ahead of the retinue. If it had been any other figure, he would summarily have instructed the rider to dismount, but seeing it was none other than the Gorkha Pönpo, he became perturbed and restless, realising that the dignity of the sovereign was at the stake. As the Dalai Lama's party came ever closer, the young courtier jumped up, seized the Gorkha Pönpo by the chest, and pulled him to the ground.

Although causing a diplomatic incident between the two countries, the 13th Dalai Lama was delighted at the audacity of the young courtier. The news of Chogyal Nyima's brave action quickly spread in the streets of Lhasa, and as his fame grew so did his rank. He later came to be known as Kashopa, and was ultimately appointed to the office of Kalon of the Tibetan Cabinet (Kashag), becoming one of the most powerful figures in Tibetan politics. It is a phenomenon of Tibetan society, that despite the strict social hierarchy and rules governing social relations, if an able individual catches the eye of the sovereign, and shows his or her worth, that person could rise up the ranks very quickly. Proof of this is that many of Tibet's aristocrats have had a humble origin.

The most famous such example is the case of Dasang Damdul Tsarong, who became one of the most charismatic and colourful figures in Tibet in the early twentieth century. In the *Who's Who in Tibet*, he is described as having occupied 'a menial position' before he rose to become one of the most powerful and controversial figures in the Tibetan politics. He spoke some Russian, Mongolian and Hindi, which he had acquired during his many travels. In 1904, as the British army under Younghusband's command marched towards Lhasa, the 13th Dalai Lama fled to Mongolia. Among those who accompanied him was the son of an arrow-maker from Penpo, named Nangang because he was born on the eve of the New Year – Losar. Nangang soon became one of the Chensel, a title meaning 'shining brightly before the sovereign's eyes'.

Nangang's rise to the peak of Tibetan political and social circles is narrated in an epic fashion. It is said that when, in 1910, the 13th Dalai Lama once again fled after a Chinese army invaded Lhasa, Nangang and sixty men under his command diverted the Chinese army from their pursuit of the Dalai Lama by holding them off at Chaksam, the iron bridge over the Tsangpo river. Later, Nangang escaped to India disguised as a post carrier under the nose of the Chinese who had already secured the border areas. On his reutrn to Lhasa nine months later, the Dalai Lama appointed Nangang as the Military Commander and gave him the responsibility of creating a new modern army. He later married into the aristocratic Tsarong family and assumed their name. Frederick Spencer Chapman, who formed part of the British Mission to Lhasa of 1936, describes him as the 'strong man of Lhasa'.[9] The *Who's Who* identifies him as 'very pro-British', and Basil Gould remembers Tsarong telling him that the British presence in Lhasa is 'like the shade of a great tree in a dry land'.[10]

Dasang Damdul Tsarong in His House
Frederick Spencer Chapman, 1936–1937

Dasang Damdul Tsarong sitting in the altar room of his recently-built house in Lhasa, where members of the 1936 Mission were often invited. Spencer Chapman describes it thus: 'We had tea in the private chapel, which is the largest and finest room in the house.' (1938:104–5). Tsarong occupies the throne normally allocated to visiting incarnate lamas.
PRM 1998.131.680.

Tsarong's story is another example of the way that Tibetan society was not governed by a rigid caste system. As the Tibetan saying goes, 'if a son has the ability, the throne of Ganden is for him to take'.[11]

What is demonstrated by these anecdotes is that Lhasa was much more than a city to which foreigners came to marvel; it was the centre of the Tibetan world where fortunes were made and ambitious men acquired power. At the time of the 13th Dalai Lama, people like Kashopa and Tsarong rose from the lowest strata to take on pivotal roles in Tibetan politics. Even in the religious field, ordinary monks from Mongolia and other parts of the Tibetan cultural world flocked to study at the three largest monasteries near Lhasa, which served as great centres of learning. Monks, no matter how humble or remote their origin, could establish reputations as scholars and obtain great religious authority. In places like Amdo in northeastern Tibet, monks returning from studies in Lhasa acquired special status and prestige.

For the British, the attraction of Lhasa was not simply its romantic allure as the capital of Shangri-La, but they recognised that it also functioned as Tibet's seat of power. The Chinese and Nepalese, as noted earlier, had a strong presence in the city. The Manchu Qing dynasty (1644–1911) which had conquered China in the mid-17th century, had taken an early interest in Tibet and had by the eighteenth century established their representative, the Amban, in the city. However, with the collapse of the Qing, the Amban's office was expelled from Lhasa in 1911 and for nearly three decades the Chinese lost all its influence in Tibet. It appeared that the Tibetans were determined to keep it that way. The Nationalist Guomingdang, who ultimately took the reins of government after the collapse of the Qing, made repeated attempts to gain some measure of influence in Tibet, but Tibetan resistance and their lack of authority in much of China meant that their efforts failed. By the second decade of the twentieth century, therefore, the only other real contender amongst the foreign representatives in Lhasa were the Nepalese.

A City in Transformation

In the early 1930s, Lhasa was being electrified and some of the wealthy aristocrats began to import electrical generators and other foreign goods. Chang Ngopa Ringang, who had been sent to England in 1913 by the 13th Dalai Lama, returned to Lhasa in 1924 after qualifying as an electrical engineer. Ringang would proudly sign after his name ACGI (Associate of the City Guild Institute), which later became the Imperial College of the University of London. (Ringang could claim to be the first graduate in the whole of Tibet.) The 13th Dalai Lama imported two cars, with number plates 'Tibet 1' and 'Tibet 2'. During this period, more than at any other time in Tibet's history, Lhasa's material culture was being transformed by the novelty of having a ready availability of a large array of foreign-made goods, imported exclusively from India. The Tibetan language also altered, with numerous new words filtering into common usage. This indicates that changes were not only confined to the upper circles of Tibetan society, but widespread at least in places like Lhasa, Shigatse and Gyantse. The everyday use of foreign words in the language also shows that Tibet was far from being the isolated and forbidden land of popular perception. The mode of dress began to change and terms such as *pa ki* (pocket), *cot* (coat), *pa du lu* (pantalon), *ka mis* (chemise) and *jur ta* (leather shoe) entered the language. In addition, *shig ras* (cigarettes), *mo ta* (motor), *re li* (train), *be si kob* (bioscope) and *dar tshan* (dozen) made their first appearance. People began to invent new names for foreign objects. The Tibetan word for bicycle is *kang-ghari*, which is made up of *kang* (*rkang*) meaning foot and attaching the Hindi word *ghari* (vehicle) after the first syllable. Similarly, the new term for cement is made up of *bhi la* from Blighty and the suffix *sa* meaning earth or soil. Thus, cement is known in Tibetan as 'English soil'. (This could also be translated as 'foreign soil', as the English term Blighty is ultimately from Hindi *bilayati* for foreign land.) The word for motorbike is even more inventive, and drawing on the

Jigme Taring and Yuthok Tashi Dhundup in Army Uniform
Frederick Spencer Chapman, 1936–1937

Taring and Yuthok in their new Depön (General) uniforms. These were inspired by British models and included khaki tunics, riding breeches and field boots. As both were members of noble families, they wear long turquoise ear-rings and amulets under their hats. This photograph was taken at a military display designed to illustrate the quality of the Tibetan forces to Colonel Neame (the 1936 Mission's military advisor). A large crowd turned out for this display and the band played 'God Save the Queen'.
PRM 1998.131.501.

sound made by the bikes, the Tibetans simply called it '*bag ba*'. Even more surprising is the use of the term '*ku kru ma ni*' (a mispronunciation of the English 'good morning') which became so widespread that it even entered the lyrics of popular songs of the time. [12]

Photography became one of the favourite fashionable pastimes of the wealthy, and many aristocrats began to purchase cameras. The negatives were sent all the way to Calcutta for developing. Later people like George Tsarong and Demo Rinpoche, a nephew of the 13th Dalai Lama, were keen photographers and had dark rooms in their houses. In fact, the camera had entered Tibet at the beginning of the twentieth century, when Tibetans began to capture and compose their own images. In 1918, when Chinese and Tibetans clashed in Kham, Albert Shelton, an American missionary based in Bathang noted in his autobiography that two of the Tibetan generals who defeated the Chinese recorded their victory on film.[13] Many of these early images taken by Tibetans were destroyed during the Cultural Revolution, when the Red Guards saw the possession of a camera and photographs as a sign of decadence and imperialism. One of the earliest surviving collections of photographs by a Tibetan is that of Demo Rinpoche, who first acquired a camera in 1925 from a Newar merchant in Lhasa. In 1976, the Red Guards subjected him to a public struggle session (*thamzing*) and paraded him through the streets of Lhasa. A photograph of the incident shows him with a camera hanging round his neck, which was presumably intended to humiliate him further.[14]

When we compare the photographs by the Tibetans themselves to those by Westerners, there is a clear contrast. One image in Demo's collection shows him on his bed, with his wife resting her head on his lap. She is relaxed and comfortable, not even looking toward the camera. Demo has his right arm protectively around her shoulder and is looking directly at the camera. They are both dressed casually with no sign or display of wealth or ostentation – the wall behind is bare; the cupboard by the side of the bed is empty.[15] In Tibetan photographs, such as those by George Tsarong and Demo, one sees fewer significant objects or landmarks, their pictures document personal history and self representation.[16] The value of Tibetan photographs lies in the personal history of their subjects and their representation of Lhasa not as a static place fixed in time, but as a location that is changing and shifting before the photographers' eyes. Demo's photographs show the construction of his new residence and George Tsarong captures the laying of a water pipeline in Lhasa and construction works. Of course, these are still unusual pictures even by Tibetan standards.

At this time Ladhaki Muslims and Newari merchants also saw the opportunity to profit from the craze for photography and opened the first photographic studios in Lhasa in the 1940s, where families and other groups could be photographed. The studio often had background scenery depicting a foreign landscape, usually the alpine terrain of Kashmir, attesting to Indian influences. The sitter would pose with suitable objects such as plastic flowers placed strategically in the foreground. One of the favourite props was the bicycle. Lhasa residents often went to have their photographs taken just before the New Year celebrations, with new costumes and jewellery made for the occasion. Going to the studio was not a private affair but a family or group ritual. The finished photographs were prominently displayed in peoples' homes and guests were invited to view these images which projected a sense of a modern Tibetan family.

Kanwal Krishna's Portraits

In 1933, the 13th Dalai Lama passed away and in 1940, the new Dalai Lama was enthroned in the Potala Palace. As in England, a new era is marked by a change in monarch, the succession of the Dalai Lama shapes the era. The reign of the 13th Dalai Lama had

Kanwal Krishna Painting a Portrait of Reting Rinpoche, the Regent of Tibet
Photographer unknown, 1940

Kanwal Krishna with his sketchbook (far left), an unidentified Tibetan and the Regent of Tibet, Reting Rinpoche, in full monastic robes seated on his throne. Courtesy of Chitrangada Sharma.

Tsenzhab Kyutsang Jampa Mönlam
Kanwal Krishna, 1940

Said to be a brilliant monk, Tsenzhab Kyutsang Jampa Mönlam became the 17th abbot of Sera Je, one of the colleges of Sera monastery. He had been the debating partner (tsenzhab) *of the 13th Dalai Lama, and thus it became one of his titles. In 1936, the Regent, Reting, appointed him as the ecclesiastical head of the search party for the 14th Dalai Lama who was found in Taktse in Amdo. In 1940, he was appointed third of a group of three tutors to the 14th Dalai Lama. In his autobiography the 14th Dalai Lama writes, 'I was particularly fond of Kewtsang* (sic.) *Rinpoche. Like myself, he was from Amdo. He was so kind that I could never take him seriously. During our lessons, instead of reciting what I was supposed to, I used to hang round his neck and say, "You recite".' (Dalai Lama 1990:19)*
Private Collection.

been one of the most critical periods in Tibet's history, the country having been exposed to threats both from the east and the south and having made its first steps towards modernising and opening up to the West. By the time of the 14th Dalai Lama's Installation ceremony, the world was engulfed in war. It might have been supposed that neither the Chinese nor the British would have much interest in events in Lhasa. However, this was not the case, and the British and the Chinese were both present, and debate raged as to which party should have more prominence at the ceremony. Historians today continue to comb over the facts, trying to determine whether it was the Chinese or the British delegates who had a better position.

This debate has overshadowed many other features of the Installation ceremony. Among Basil Gould's British delegation was a well-known Indian artist, Kanwal Krishna. He had studied at the Government School of Art and Crafts in Calcutta, which under the directorship of Percy Brown, produced and shaped a whole generation of Indian modernist artists, of which Kanwal was a prominent

Khemed Sonam Wangdi
Kanwal Krishna, 1940

Khemed (1902–1975) was born into the Surkhang family, but married into the Kunsangtse family as a magpa, *which meant that he lived with his wife's famiy and assumed their name. He served as Dzongpön (District Magistrate) of Tselha gang and served as a Depön (General of the Dalai Lama's body guard regiment) in the Tibetan army, after having received British training in the Indian army. In 1936, Khemed was appointed as the secular head of the search party for the new (14th) incarnation of the Dalai Lama. In 1939, Khemed served as Laja, an important post traditionally held by a secular official, serving in conjunction with two ecclesiastic officials. The Laja is the equivalent of the Chancellor of the Exchequer, overseeing the government's income and expenditure. Khemed was said to be critical of the Regent Reting's use of government loans for private business conducted on his personal estate. Khemed, therefore, refused to sanction a government loan to Reting, who thereupon had him dismissed from government service, citing in explanation that Khemed had once left Lhasa without informing the Regent's office – a minor infringement of the rules. In 1940, Khemed was appointed as the liaison officer by Reting to receive Basil Gould and the British delegation. After 1942, under the new Regent, Taktra, he was reinstated as a government official and in 1946 was the head of the Tibetan delegation that travelled to India and China to congratulate the British and Allies for their victory in the Second World War. In 1951, Khemed was a member of the Tibetan delegation that signed the 17 Point Agreement with China.*
Private Collection.

Phünkang Jetrungla
Kanwal Krishna, 1940

Son of Phünkang Tashi Dorji, Jetrungla (1918–after 1947) served as a tse-drung *(monk official) in the government. Although he never occupied any high position, Jetrungla was widely considered to be the Regent Reting's lover and companion. When Reting was imprisoned in 1947, the Regent Taktra tried to remove him from Lhasa by offering him a post in China. Instead Jetrungla left Lhasa for Sikkim.*
Private Collection.

Deki Dolkar
Kanwal Krishna, 1940

Born in Taktse village in Amdo, Deki Dolkar (1931?–1982) came to Lhasa as an intended bride for the 14th Dalai Lama's brother Gyalo Dhondhup. Once in Lhasa he refused to marry her. However, Deki Dolkar stayed in Lhasa and managed an estate belonging to the Dalai Lama's family. She remained in Tibet after 1959 but was persecuted during the Cultural Revolution (1966–1976) because of her connection to the Dalai Lama's family.
Private Collection.

Yabzhi Phünkang Tashi Dorje
Kanwal Krishna, 1940

In 1938 Phünkang was appointed a Kalon of the Tibetan Cabinet (Kashag) by the Regent Reting, allegededly because his son, Phünkang Jetrungla, was Reting's lover. He was, therefore, regarded as a strong supporter of Reting Rinpoche. In 1945, after Reting's removal from the regency, Phünkang's wife was accused of spreading rumours that the new Regent, Taktra, was having an affair with a well-known Lhasa prostitute. Taktra dismissed Phünkang from the Kashag, and later Phünkang was implicated in Reting's attempt in 1947 to overthrow Taktra, arrested and imprisoned for several months.
Private Collection.

example. Kanwal had accompanied the famous Indian nationalist and Buddhist scholar Rahul Sankratayan on a trip to western Tibet in 1936, during which they were also joined by the Tibetan savant Gedhun Chonphel (whose portrait Kanwal painted). After his return to India, an exhibition was held in Calcutta of Kanwal's western Tibetan paintings, attracting the attention of many senior colonial officers who were impressed by his work. In the same year, Lady Linlithgow, wife of the then Viceroy of India, visited Bhutan and Sikkim, and expressed her further desire to travel to Tibet. The Government of India felt that it was too arduous a trip for her Ladyship to make and instead decided to conjure up a vision of Tibet to be unveiled before her Ladyship's eyes – in the form of paintings by Kanwal Krishna. He was duly commissioned to travel to Tibet and for an exhibition of his paintings to be held in Gangtok (Sikkim). After the exhibition, Lady Linlithgow wrote in the artist's notebook: 'I think Mr Krishna's work is extremely good. He has a great sense of colour and design. I have bought some of the sketches.' Lady Linlithgow was herself a keen amateur painter – (Kanwal described her as a 'Sunday painter'). Kanwal was therefore asked to accompany her on a painting trip to Dromo in Tibet in September 1939. While there, Kanwal recalls: 'When I was sitting at the dinner table with her in the Chumbi Valley, a telegram was received to say the new Dalai Lama was moving to Lhasa. I immediately said I wish I could be there. She said, "why not?" That, from the lips of the Vicereine, was an intention of her will. So my appointment was fixed.'[17]

As much of the rest of the world focused on the war, Tibet remained aloof and unruffled by the larger events outside. In hindsight, the irony is that neither the Tibetans nor the British were to know they were participating in the end of an era. The British Empire ended in 1947 and two years later Tibet lost her independence to China. Perhaps, it was due to a sense of premonition of the significance of the moment that the British decided to record the Installation ceremony and courtly life of Lhasa so accurately. Basil Gould's report to his government is meticulous in its detail and both he (and some Tibetans) recorded the ceremony in colour film. Meanwhile, Kanwal Krishna was commissioned by Gould to paint a portrait of the young Dalai Lama to mark the occasion. Thrilled to be in Tibet's capital, Kanwal later told a reporter, 'I saw the street procession as the [the Dalai Lama] entered Lhasa. People talk about the colours of Rajasthan, but they fade in comparison.' During the ceremony, Kanwal made a water-colour portrait of the Dalai Lama, took photographs of the throne, and later worked on a canvas to produce an oil painting of the newly enthroned pontiff for the government of British India. Later, the painting was hung on a wall of the office of the Political Officer in Gangtok.

At this time in Tibet, there was no tradition of portrait painting in the Western realist style, instead there was the centuries-old tradition of *thangka* painting which included portraits of great lamas, their disiciples and secular patrons in a highly stylized manner. Kanwal's paintings therefore differed in both their style and compostion from anything that had existed in Tibet before. Perhaps the popularity of photography among the nobility and, more importantly, the widespread distribution of photographs of the 13th Dalai Lama, had led to a change in notions about how a subject could be represented.[18] The idea of capturing a likeness constituted the modern. Even today, among Tibetans, the idea of modern art is characterised by a realistic depiction of a subject. During his stay in Lhasa, Kanwal Krishna attracted the interest of the Tibetan nobility through his personal charm and artistic talent. Realizing that they were engaged in a great moment in history, they wished to be recorded in their finest regalia. Kanwal made over seventy portraits of Tibetan officials. As an artist, he was attracted by the colour and splendour of the enthronement and the New Year (Losar) and Mönlam Prayer festivities which followed soon after. He was given unprecedented access during his stay in Lhasa, as he was not only a member of the British delegation, but also his paintings were a novelty in Lhasa. Since he was doing watercolours he could do a portrait very quickly, and he often made copies for his sitters. Therefore, many aristocratic families had Kanwal's paintings in their houses. This was probably the first time that Tibetans began to display Western-style portraiture in their houses.

Portraits: The Dalai Lama's Family

Deki Tsering (opposite)
Kanwal Krishna, 1940

Née Sonam, Deki Tsering (1901–1981) was the mother of the 14th Dalai Lama, and whom Basil Gould described as 'one in a million'. She is often referred to by the honorific title of Gyayum Chenmo (Great Mother). The Dalai Lama described her in his autobiography as 'one of the kindest people I have known. She was truly wonderful and was loved by all who knew her.' (Dalai Lama 1990:8)
Private Collection.

It was natural for Kanwal to want to paint the young Dalai Lama's parents, his father Chökhong and his mother Deki Tsering. After the enthronement of their son as the sovereign of Tibet, the Dalai Lama's family is ennobled as Yabzhi, a title literally meaning 'the father's estate'. Since the eighteenth century, the Yabzhis have constituted the highest ranks of Tibetan aristocracy. The 14th Dalai Lama's family is known as the Yabzhi Takla. Kanwal recalls, 'When I painted his [the Dalai Lama's] mother, it was in an ante-room [of the Potala Palace]. He was [in the room] and very excited and curious, he kept sending attendants to check on [the] progress. When some

達賴佛母親覽安都
16.3.40
LHASA

Chökhong Tsering
Kanwal Krishna, 1940

The father of the 14th Dalai Lama, Chökhong Tsering (d. 1945) was given on his son's accession the title of Kung, and is often referred to as Gyayab (Great Father). The Dalai Lama in his autobiography writes, 'My father was a man of medium height with a very quick temper. I remember pulling at his moustache once and being hit hard for my trouble.' (Dalai Lama 1990:7–8) He was fond of horses and the Dalai Lama recalls that he had a reputation as a healer of horses in the family's home in Taktse in Amdo. He died of illness in 1945, although there are some that believe he was poisoned because of his close friendship with the Regent, Reting.
Private Collection.

Gyalo Dhondhup (opposite left)
Kanwal Krishna, 1940

The eldest brother of the 14th Dalai Lama. Gyalo Dhondhup (b. 1928) went to China in 1944 to study and escaped to India after the establishment of the Communist Government. In India he was actively involved in organising the Tibetan resistance movement and arranged clandestine contact with the American Central Intelligence Agency, and the CIA's covert operation in Tibet between 1957–1972 was managed under his leadership. In 1979, he met with the Chinese leader Deng Xiaoping and initiated new negotiations between the Chinese government and the Dalai Lama. Gyalo Dhondhup is regarded as one of the most influential figures in Tibetan political affairs today.
Private Collection.

likeness was there I sent the painting in to him and he returned it with a plate of cakes.' In the two portraits, the sovereign's parents display some unease in their posture, their costumes being newly made and their sitting postions seem uncomfortable. The faces are stern and the design of their clothes is not in the usual style of Lhasa aristocracy, but are a mixture of Manchu and Tibetan garments meshed to create an air of royalty. Tibetan accounts and reports submitted from the Dekyi Lingka speak of the Dalai Lama's father's excessive demands for material and privileges befitting his status. He was said to be hot-tempered while the 'Great Mother' was said to be gentle and gracious.

Basil Gould, in a report, describes them in a more intimate manner than Tibetans ever would: 'The father is a man of quiet and gentle pose, with a serious face on which smiles go "out and in". The mother is surely one in a million, the worthy mother of a Dalai Lama.' A street song contrasted the temperaments of the parents. It went something like this:

The Great Father Chökhong Tsering,
Is in a trance, like an oracle,
The Great Mother Jetsun Dolma,
Sits [calmly] on the altar.[19]

These Lhasa street songs are like newspaper cartoons in the West, providing a succinct commentary on political and social events of the day. In this case, the song plays on the name of the Dalai Lama's father. Line one uses his first name Chökhong, which has the same meaning as the protective deity and is often associated with wrathfulness, while the mother is compared to the goddess Tara, resting peacefully still on an altar.

Lobzang Samten (below right)
Kanwal Krishna, 1940

An elder brother of the Dalai Lama, until he was eight years old Lobzang Samten (1933–1985) was brought up in the Potala Palace as companion to his younger brother. The Dalai Lama wrote of him, 'I was about eight when Lobzang Samten was sent to study at a private school. Naturally, this saddened me for he was my sole contact with my family.... I only saw him during the school holiday at the time of the full moon. When he left after each visit, I remember standing at the window watching, my heart full of sorrow, as he disappeared in the distance.' (Dalai Lama 1990:21) After coming to exile in India, he was the head of the Tibetan Medical Institute in Dharamsala. In 1979, he led the first Tibetan delegation to China and Tibet after Deng Xiaoping opened dialogue with the Dalai Lama.
Private Collection.

The Regent of Tibet in His Reception Chamber
Frederick Spencer Chapman, 1936–1937
PRM 1998.131.516.

The Regent

Between the time when the British first established their Mission in Lhasa in 1936 and 1947 when the Union Jack was lowered and replaced by the flag of India, the Dalai Lama was in his minority and Tibet was ruled by regents, appointed by the Tibetan General Assembly. Hence, ever since the establishment of the rule of the Dalai Lamas, the regent has always been a powerful figure in Tibetan history. While Tibetans and Westerners alike assume that the Dalai Lamas ruled Tibet, in fact for the vast majority of the time since the eighteenth century regents governed the country.[20] Political factions that formed around various candidates for the regency were the main cause of political strife in the Tibet of this period. After the death of the 13th Dalai Lama, and until a year after the enthronement of the 14th Dalai Lama, the regent was Reting Rinpoche. Affectionately remembered by the present Dalai Lama, who recalls: 'I came to like him very much. His most striking feature, I remember, was a continually blocked nose. As a person, he was quite imaginative, with a very relaxed mental disposition, a man who took things easily. He loved picnics and horses.'[21]

Kanwal made a watercolour portrait of Regent Reting sitting on a bed in his summer residence and wearing a richly decorated silk brocade costume. In 1936, Spencer Chapman had taken a photograph of the Regent at exactly the same location, and the photograph was later reproduced in his book, *Lhasa; the Holy City*. In the photo, he is dressed in an ordinary monk's robe, while in Kanwal's painting he is dressed in a layman's yellow brocade coat over a maroon *chuba* (robe). The colour is bright, detracting attention from his small body and giving an air of distance. His posture is composed and there is stiffness in his expression. The table in the foreground is the same in both the painting and the photograph, with a spittoon in the same position on the far left hand side of the table and the teacup with silver holders and inkpot stand on the left. Reting's residence was renowned for its ostentatious display of wealth, which is reflected in the painting's background detail. His estate (*labrang)* saw the regency as an opportunity to accrue huge wealth for Reting monastery, and the Reting *labrang* became a major commercial enterprise controlling the profitable Indo-Tibetan trade. During the 1930s and 1940s, the three largest Tibetan merchants who virtually held a monopoly over Tibet's trade were known as *Ra sa pon sum*. The '*ra*' referred to Reting, '*sa*' to Sudhutsang – a Khampa trading family, and '*pon*' to Pomdatsang, perhaps the largest of the three.

Reting Rinpoche
Kanwal Krishna, 1940

Thupten Jamphel Yeshi Tenpai Gyaltsen (1912–1947) was born into a humble household, but at an early age was recognised as the 5th incarnation of the Reting Rinpoche. He studied at Sera monastery and was awarded one of the highest monastic degrees, the Geshe Lharampa, in front of the 13th Dalai Lama. In 1934, at the age of 22, he became the Regent of Tibet. In 1941 Reting was forced to resign as the Regent and handed the regentship to Taktra. It was rumoured that Reting had made a secret agreement with Taktra that after few years Reting would resume as the Regent. However, in 1947 when Taktra persisted in refusing to relinquish the office, Reting and his supporters attempted to overthrow him. The coup was unsuccessful, and Reting was arrested and imprisoned. He died in prison, and it is most likely that he was murdered.
Private Collection.

The Palace of Reting Rinpoche, the Regent of Tibet
Frederick Spencer Chapman, 1936–1937
PRM 1998.131.512.

The Reting *labrang*'s aggrandizement attracted public criticism and many satirical songs critical of the Regent appeared in the streets of Lhasa. The verse below was posted on the walls of the Barkhor district:

The wolves on the plain are contented,
The fox between the two rivers is satisfied,
The Regent who has eaten a mountain
Cannot quench his thirst even after drinking an ocean.[22]

Despite the general criticism, the public tended to excuse the lama himself for the excess and blamed the *labrang changdzo* – the estate manager. However, there was one charge that the Reting could not avoid. The frail and small-framed Reting Rinpoche was known within courtly circles for his avaricious sexual appetite for both male and female lovers. In 1941, the young Dalai Lama was approaching the age when he had to take the novice monk's vow. According to Buddhist tradition, the vow must be administered by a lama who himself was not an apostate. Clearly, a large sector of the public and religious community was worried about this situation. While the public could stomach the accumulation of wealth, this was an entirely different matter; it concerned the religious status of the Dalai Lama. Reting was forced to resign and hand over power to Taktra Rinpoche whom the Reting had previously appointed as one of the three tutors to the young Dalai Lama. In 1947, the ex-Regent Reting was accused of attempting to stage a *coup d'état*. The story of the feud between the supporters of Taktra and Reting is worthy of Shakespearean historical drama. Reting Rinpoche died in prison. Some say he was poisoned, others say he was suffocated and still others claim he was put to death by crushing his testicles.

Since Kanwal was using water-colours, and could finish the work in one or two hours, he could ask the sitter to fix their signature and seal to the completed painting. All the Tibetans who sat for him also wrote comments in the artist's notebook. It is notable that all the Tibetans wrote similar comments and used phrases such as 'just like' (*dngos gsum*) and expressions of amazement (*ha las pa*). When Kanwal finished his painting of Reting, he showed it to him. Reting wrote the following comment in his neat handwriting in the artist's notebook: 'After arriving in Lhasa Mr Krishna Kanwal performed magical tricks and showed me his paintings of landscapes and peoples. The paintings are just like real life and amazed everyone.'

The Nechung Oracle

Kanwal also painted the Nechung Oracle – or Nechung Kuden, Lobzang Namgye. A few years ago, I visited the Nechung monastery re-established in Dharamsala and showed a photograph of the portrait of the Nechung Oracle to some older monks. One elderly monk immediately recalled that the painting was done by the Indian *jadoo wallah* (magician) who visited the monastery; he even remembered the day when Kanwal

The Nechung Oracle
Kanwal Krishna, 1940
Private Collection.

came to the monastery. Although the Nechung Oracle did not exercise any direct political power, his divine guidance was frequently sought by the Tibetan government and the Dalai Lama. Nechung was the highest-ranking in the Tibetan pantheon of spirits, and the Nechung Oracle designated to be the spirit's medium was known as a *kuden* (*sku bsten*) – the physical manifestation of the spirit. Therefore, the British always maintained a cordial relationship with Nechung monastery and whenever British officials came to Lhasa, they made a courtesy call to the monastery. At the time of Gould's visit in 1936 and during the enthronement ceremony of the 14th Dalai Lama in 1940, the Nechung Oracle was a monk named Lobzang Namgyal (1894– 1945). He was an impressive figure with an imposing presence, described in *Who's Who* as 'an intelligent, friendly and sociable monk.' In Kanwal's painting we see him on a raised seat, where high officials are generally received in Nechung monastery. His broad face with a pencilled moustache stares directly at the observer. On the table before him is a tea cup and beside it stand a gold and jewel-encrusted ceremonial cup of Nechung. The portrait took Kanwal just two hours.

Kyibu and Ringang

The enthronement ceremony of the Dalai Lama took place just before the Tibetan Losar (New Year) and the *Mönlam* Prayer Festival, which takes place at the anniversary of the death and birth of Tsongkapa (1357–1419), the founder of Geluk school of Tibetan Buddhism. Two young Tibetan officials, who frequently acted as translators for the British with the Tibetan government, were actively involved in organising the *Mönlam* ceremony in 1940. Basil Gould had known both of these young Tibetan officials since their teens – as they had come to England in 1913 to be educated at Rugby. Soon after the 13th Dalai Lama had returned to Lhasa from exile in India, he decided to send four boys for schooling in England. Two of the boys were Kyibu Wangdu Norbhu and Chang Ngopa Rigzin Dorje commonly known as Ringang. Ringang excelled in his studies at Rugby and, as noted earlier, went on to graduate in electrical engineering and return to Tibet in 1924 and set about installing electricity in Lhasa. Kyibu was less successful in his schooling and had difficulty adjusting to school life in England. He returned to Lhasa in 1917, and trained in map-making and agriculture, and spent a great deal of time on his estates.

Ringang
Kanwal Krishna, 1940
Private Collection.

Kanwal's portrait of Ringang shows him sitting on a Western style chair wearing a ceremonial costume of a Yasö General. The dress indicates that the painting was carried out during the *Mönlam* Festival. Shortly after the *Mönlam*, a military display is held in Lhasa for the public, said to have been instituted by the 5th Dalai Lama (1617–1682) to mark the defeat of the Tsangpa Kings in 1642 by the soldiers of Gushri Khan (1582–1655). The display is led by two officials known as Yasö Chikyab, or Generals. In 1940, Ringang had been appointed as one of these two officials, and the position of the

The Yasö General, Ruthog Depön
Hugh Richardson, *c.* 1936–1950

The Yasö General, Ruthog Depön, and two attendants. The Yasö Generals are commanders of an ancient Tibetan militia whose elaborate dress could be so heavy that they could not stand up (according to Richardson). Only fourth rank officials were allowed to take this role, and those who performed it incurred great expense when ordering the fine gowns required. In 1940, Ringang was made a Yasö General and Dundul Namgyal (George) Tsarong became one later.
PRM 2001.59.9.73.1.

Yasö Chikyab – although purely ceremonial, was an important and costly one for his family. In Tibet, the aristocracy formed the core of the government civil service. Known as the *drungkor*, they were unpaid and their expenses had to be met from estates granted to them by the government.

The position of Yasö Chikyab, commanding 500 men who wore the uniform of the ancient Mongol army, was held annually and the main expense was the costly costume to be worn during the ceremonies. While the dress could be hired from relatives who had served as Yasö before, it was a matter of prestige for each family to be able to produce their own ceremonial costume. The costume Ringang is wearing, therefore had to be made especially for the occasion and is made from yellow embroidered silk brocade with sleeves lined with fox fur. On the shoulder, a soft fox fur is attached loosely and the outfit is topped by a round hat known as *wogor*, also made from fox fur.

Ringang at this period was a 4th rank official and acted as English translator for the Tibetan Cabinet (Kashag) and the Regent. As one of the few people in Tibet who had traveled and been educated in the West, he was in great demand not only as a translator but also in his capacity of maintaining the electricty supply for the city. In 1942, when the Regent Taktra established a foreign office under the Kashag, Ringang was one of the first secretaries of the office.

Another outfit worn only during the New Year ceremony was known as *gyaluche* (literally meaning 'king's dress'). These costumes,

Kyibu
Kanwal Krishna, 1940
Private Collection.

which were only worn during the New Year celebrations and usually kept in the treasury at Potala Palace, were said to belong to the ancient kings of Tibet. Kanwal's painting of Kyibu shows him wearing a *gyaluche* costume, although less elaborate than the ones kept in the Potala Palace. In 1940, Kyibu held the position of Mipön, a post similar to both that of mayor and city magistrate. All civil or criminal disputes in Lhasa were brought before the Mipön's office. The Mipön was also the head of a small Lhasa police force, which had been established by the 13th Dalai Lama in 1922 and trained by British advisors to the Indian police.

Tenthong

Among the officials who sat for Kanwal is Tenthong Tomjor Wangchuk, the son of the Shapé of the Tibetan Cabinet, Tenthong Gyurme Gyatso. Kanwal's portrait shows the younger Tenthong sitting on a raised seat in his family home. He is wearing a long *sog gil* ear-ring that can only be worn by sons of aristocracy and a yellow hat known as a *boto*, which signifies that the wearer is a junior official. On first joining the government service, the young aristocrat wears a *boto* and a long silk *chuba*. Tenthong Tomjor at the time was only 18 or 19, and said to be very bright – learning Chinese and English from members of the British and Chinese missions.

The 1930s and 1940s were perhaps one of the must turbulent periods in the recent history of Tibet in terms of internal conflict and external pressure from China. It was a time when some younger Tibetans were being exposed to new ideas and the need for reforms in the country was beginning to be recognised. In 1943, a group of Khampas from Bathang arrived in Lhasa, among them Baba Phuntsog Wangyal and Ngawang Kalsang, who had been educated in China and attracted to communism. They had come to Lhasa with the hope of raising support from the government to oppose the Chinese warlord Liu Wenhui who ruled much of Kham. Phuntsog Wangyal and Ngawang Kalsang had an even more daring idea – to establish contact with progressive Tibetans and set up a Communist Party. One of the people who was receptive to the idea was Tomjor. The young radicals would meet clandestinely at the Tenthong mansion to discuss ways to unite Tibet and promote reforms. In 1943 they established the United Tibet Communist Party.[23] It was never likely that this group would have made a radical impact in Tibet, but the fact that it existed at all indicates that new and radical ideas were being seriously considered by

Two Men and Crowd at New Year
(opposite)
Hugh Richardson, *c.* 1947

In front, Kyibu and Dundul Namgyal Tsarong (son of Dasang Damdul Tsarong, the close friend of the 1936 Mission) wearing the ringyen *(ancient precious ornaments) at New Year. According to the junior Tsarong, 'The Tibetan government preserved these costumes very carefully, and they were stored in the Namsey-Genzoe, the treasury at the Potala Palace. They were taken out every year and on special occasions by the council of ministers together with the Dalai Lama's representative. There had been occasions when the Dalai Lama was personally present during the opening of the Namsey Genzoe. Traditional custom imposed on junior officials the duty of wearing these costumes during the New Year's festival ... The officials, whose turn was shown on a list, were called upon to take delivery of the costumes one day before the ceremony. Items were delivered one by one with a detailed list of the costumes with precious ornaments. Even cracked or chipped stones were recorded on the list. After the ceremony, they were taken back, making sure that everything was intact. If damage or loss of any part was found, the wearer was responsible for replacing them. If someone had lost turquoises, they sometimes had to get into debt to replace them.' (1995:125) In this photograph, the jewels are wrapped in a kind of cloth sling perhaps to reduce the risk of losing them. Richardson's photograph was probably taken in 1947 – suggesting that Kyibu performed this role a number of times as he was also photographed by Spencer Chapman at New Year in 1937.*
PRM 2001.59.18.16.1.

Tenthong Tomjor Wangchuk
Kanwal Krishna, 1940
Private Collection.

Tibetan intellectuals at the time. The existence of the group had to be kept secret from the Tibetan government and from the British, who would have certainly regarded this as dangerous. As we know, communism as brought to Tibet by the Chinese proved fatal and destructive.

The Aftermath

In 1947, the British left India and their imperial interest in Tibet ended. Hugh Richardson, who had been the longest-serving head of the British Mission in Lhasa, became the head of the Indian Mission. He left Lhasa early in 1950, thus ending the British link with Tibet first established by Warren Hastings in 1774. British–Tibet relations underwent three main phases. The first phase of the relationship occurred between 1774–1903, when the Tibetans strongly resisted any attempts by the British to enter Tibet. The second period lasted from 1904 10 1936, which was a time of building trust and confidence. The final period, as recorded in Kanwal's portraits of the Tibetan aristocracy, lasted for a decade until 1947. By then it had become evident that Tibet and Britain enjoyed a close relationship, which led to many intimate and genuine cross-cultural friendships. Tibetans, like many people, often ponder the 'what ifs' of history, contemplating how the fate of Tibet may have been different. Today a favourite conversational topic is what would have happened if the British, after reaching Lhasa in 1904, had established control of Tibet. Such thoughts often become an expression of nostalgia for a lost opportunity.

For the British Mission, their presence in the city afforded them their best opportunity to persuade the Tibetans to look on Britain as their natural ally. Therefore, the role of the British Mission was not only to fly the flag, but also to attract the Tibetan elite in friendship in the hopes of establishing a strategic partnership. The parties and films shows at the Dekyi Linka were designed with this in the mind. And for the Tibetan, part of the glamour of the Dekyi Lingka was that it represented to the Tibetans a window on the outside world. A Tibetan who saw the films later wrote: 'from these films we got an idea of what houses in European countries looked like and what cars, aeroplanes, railways and ships were.'[24] Charlie Chaplin, Rin Tin Tin and other popular films were also shown, but most often it was British newsreel films distributed throughout the Empire that were shown at the Dekyi Lingka. During the Second World War, newsreels of British progress in the war were regularly shown at the Mission. What impressed the Tibetan nobles was not so much that the British were winning, but the insights into modern warfare and the technology – aeroplanes, war ships and tanks. Later in the 1950s, the Chinese Communists repeated the same exercise showing newsreels of the People's Liberation Army defeat of the Goumindang and anti-Japanese war. In both cases the images conveyed the power and invincibility of the exhibitor's armies.

It was not until several years after the British Mission was closed that Lhasa's first public cinema was opened, in 1953, near Shatra House in the city's Barkhor district by Yabzhi Langdün and a Muslim partner. The British had left long before and film shows were no longer confined to the select audience invited to the Dekyi Lingka. The cinema began to show Hindi films such as 'Anarkali', 'Nava Rang' and 'Awaar'. By the mid 1950s everyone from Lhasa had seen 'Awaar', a story about a vagabond and dealing with a theme of social justice. The Communists too loved the film's socio-political message. For them, the song lyrics, '*Mujhko yeh narak na chahiye; mujhko phool, mujhko geet, mujhko preet chahiye*' ('I don't want this hell; I want flowers, music and love'), were resonant of proletarian aspirations; the hell could be compared to feudal serfdom. Another film that was a great hit in Lhasa was 'Anarkali', a film about a Mughal emperor and his love for a courtesan. Almost everyone in Lhasa could hum the famous film melody '*yeh zindagi usiki hai*'. However, by 1962, India had become China's enemy and anything associated with her was considered to be dangerous. We could only watch Hindi films in the confines of the Dekyi Lingka, and once again the film shows were intended to be for the benefit of a select few. But still my brother's friends and others would sneak into the film screenings.

By the time my brother's family moved into the British Mission house (the Dekyi Lingka) in 1962, it was virtually empty. For a young Tibetan child, the Dekyi Lingka was an amazing place. It was like finding a secret garden; you step through a hidden door and a new world opened before your eyes. I remember two things most clearly about living there. An old fashioned Land Rover, in the classic limestone colour, and a movie-projector with stacks of film cans, remained in the grounds, left behind by the departing Indian staff. I don't think my brother or anyone who came to our new residence could read the captions on the cans. Therefore, no one knew in what order the reels should have been shown. But to me it did not matter which was the beginning, middle or the end. We would gather in a darkened room and watch the films being projected on a wall, with the sound of the projector humming in the background as a beam of light sprinkled with dust shone on the whitewashed wall. It was our very own cinema – and it inspired in me a lifelong love of films.

* * *

Tibet is no longer an inaccessible hidden kingdom behind the snow-capped peaks of the Himalayas. Today, thousands of tourists from all over the world flock to Lhasa, partly attracted by accounts written by British officials and their photographs. The city recorded in the images in this book is slowly disappearing and new high-rise flats are being erected where there once lay meadows. Old buildings are being pulled down to create new glass buildings. The significance and inevitability of such change was neatly and beautifully captured by that great writer on and of the British Empire, Rudyard Kipling:

Cities and Thrones and Powers,
Stand in Time's eye,
Almost as long as flowers,
Which daily die:
But, as new buds put forth,
To glad new men,
Out of the spent and unconsidered Earth,
The Cities rise again.

Rudyard Kipling, *Puck of Pook's Hill,* 1912

Notes

1. Candler 1905:308.
2. Gould 1957:207.
3. French 1994:185.
4. F. Williamson. Note on Titles and Official Ranks in Tibet. India Office Library. L/P&S/12/4185A.
5. *Who's Who in Tibet.* Calcutta, Government of India Press, 1938. L/P&S/12/418517 (India Office, Library).
6. French 1994:185.
7. Younghusband 1985:54.
8. Desideri 1971:133.
9. Chapman 1940:70.
10. Gould 1957:206.
11. Ganden monastery is the principal monastery of the Geluk school of Tibetan Buddhism
12. A Tibetan novel by Wangdor Tailing which in English would be called *The Secret of Tesurtsang* evokes the life of a well-to-do Lhasa family in the 1930s and 1940s. When the book was published in 1997, the text required extensive footnotes explaining the meanings of all the loan words from English and Hindi. See Brag gtong bkras gling dbang rdor, *Bkras zur tshang gi gsang ba'i gtam rgyud,* Tibet People's Publishing House, Lhasa, 1997.
13. Shelton 1925.
14. The photograph is published in Gao 1998.
15. The photograph is published in Gao 1998.
16. George Tsarong's photographs are published by him in Tsarong 1990. Demo's photographs are published in Gao 1998.
17. I am grateful to Jane Perkins for providing me with a transcript of an interview she conducted with Kanwal Krishina in 1990.
18. See Harris 1999; Harris 2001.
19. In Tibetan: *rgyal yab chos skyong tshe ring/ chos skyong phebs phebs phebs gis/ rgyal yum rje btsun sgrol ma/ bchod gshom nang la bzhungs shag.*
20. Goldstein 1968:166.
21. Dalai Lama 1990:18.
22. In Tibetan: *ri ma thang gi spyang ki brgyas nas 'dug,/chu gnyis bar gyi wa mo ngoms nas 'dug/ ri bo bzas nas ma 'grangs rgyal tshabs de/ rgya mtsho btungs nas ngoms pa mi 'gyur ro/.*
23. *zla ba'i shes rab. sgo ra nang pa phun tshog dbang rgyal gyi bzed rnam mdor bsdus.* Beijing 2000:4.
24. Pemba 1957:96.

Some Thoughts on Photographs as History

Elizabeth Edwards

Photographs do not in themselves preserve meanings … meaning is the result of understanding functions.

John Berger, 'The Uses of Photography', 1980.[1]

Photographs are perhaps the major historical source of the twentieth century. Yet, despite the fact that ever since the mid-nineteenth century photographs have been central to the processes of recording, preserving and disseminating information, historians have hardly begun to grasp what photographs might tell us, beyond the details they record – their forensic appearance. This short essay is an attempt to sketch out ways in which we might use photographs to think with, bringing them into the centre of our historical understanding, rather than just seeing them as some sort of ancillary window of the world – unmediated, unproblematic and illustrative of other more conventional forms of historical narrative and description. This demands that we actually engage with what photographs *are* – how do they tell us about the past? Finally, in what ways could recentering the photograph as an *object* of historical inscription impact upon the way photographs are cared for and managed within the institution, in particular here, the historical photographs of Tibet in the collections of the Pitt Rivers Museum?

Photographs are documents which are created 'by a will, for a purpose, to convey as message to an audience'[2] – the embodiment of a series of decisions encompassing the technological – which camera or film to use, the cultural or social – why a given subject is deemed 'photographable' and, closely linked to the last, the aesthetic. These decisions are informed by the intended function of the photograph and

Rooftops of Drepung Monastery (opposite)
Frederick Spencer Chapman, 1936–1937

A Sikkimese servant to the British Mission carrying a tripod on the rooftops of Drepung, the Geluk monastery located a few miles northwest of Lhasa. The founder of the Geluk school of Tibetan Buddhism, Tsongkhapa (1357–1419) is said to have taught at the site and a monastery was founded there in 1416 by his disciple Jamyang Choje Tashi Palden (1397–1449).
PRM 1998.131.360.1.

what is perceived at a given moment to be an appropriate form. For instance, perhaps the snap-shot style of photograph, such as those of resting during a journey, might imply informality or immediacy. A formal pose suggests a greater self-consciousness or interchange between subject and photographer, for instance Spencer Chapman's photographs of high-ranking officials. An aesthetic response to a subject matter, for example Richardson's photographs of the Potala, is intentionally interpretative, linking it to sets of cultural values.

While these forms, and the social relations they imply, fulfil certain expectations in relation to the usage of the photograph,

Taring Rinpoche
Frederick Spencer Chapman, 1936–1937

Taring Rinpoche (Lhatsun Rinpoche) wearing the gold-laquered papier-mâché hat used by monks when riding on horseback. An incarnate lama of Mindroling monastery, Taring Rinpoche was a high-ranking monk official and the half-brother of Raja Taring of Sikkim. At one time, he was in charge of all the monasteries in Sikkim and according to Spencer Chapman had 'the wisest and most expressive eyes in all of Asia'. He was a son of Yeshe Dolma, who later married Chogyal Tutop Namyal of Sikkim. He lived in Gangtok in Sikkim, but was expelled in 1934 and returned to Lhasa.
PRM 1998.131.490.

photographic meaning is not necessarily contained by those forms. For instance, an official portrait can, within the family, fulfil the same social function of an informal snapshot although they may have been made for very different purposes. This is because photographs transcend their original intentions and audiences. They survive into new contexts, accruing new meanings and sometimes losing old meanings beyond 'excavation'. They mediate our understanding of past, present and future. Indeed photographs carry their own future with them. For photographs inscribe, almost randomly, an infinite detail of the experienced moment in front of the camera. Such detail might come into play in the multiplicity of contexts, presenting an almost inexhaustible range of possibilities.

What *Are* Photographs?

Photographs are so ubiquitous that we seldom pause to ask ourselves what they are. However, the nature of photographs has exercised theorists and commentators on photography from its earliest days and there is still no consensus. It is easy to say what photography is not (it is not a drawing nor is it the depicted 'thing' itself), but much less easy to say for sure what it is and why it has such power.[3] Photography draws much of its power, and indeed many of its problems, from its indexicality, that is, the precise chemical trace on a negative made by light reflected off the real world in front of the camera. This 'trace' itself points to, or refers, to the very existence of the subject. Its mechanical precision appears to carry a truth value beyond that of drawing or painting. For instance, Spencer Chapman's photographs and Kanwal Krishna's paintings of the same subjects carry very different expectations and very different affective tones as representations. The photograph's authority and its sense of authenticity are grounded in this technical fact of mechanical accuracy and the cultural beliefs we bring to it.[4] This is the basis of the photograph's witnessing powers, which speak to 'claims of truth [resting] on protocols and hierarchies of evidence'[5] – it is a 'certificate of presence', it does not invent, it is authentification itself.[6] But this mechanically-produced 'witness' is comprised of fragments of space and time, of places and experiences extracted from a complex flow of life, and inscribed in chemical on paper, film or glass. By their very design photographs are meant to be reproducible, to exist in multiple copies, to move across space and time, stating 'this happened'.[7] We call these photographs.

Potala Palace
Hugh Richardson, *c.* 1936–1950

The Potala Palace was named after Mount Potalaka, the abode of the bodhisattva of compassion, Chenrezi. Known locally as Tse Podrang ('Summit Palace'), its thirteen storeys rising up from the Marpori (Red Hill) dominate the Lhasa cityscape. Constructed at the order of the 5th Dalai Lama in the mid-17th century, it was expanded during the 18th century to become one of the world's tallest buildings. The building performed multiple functions as the winter home of the Dalai Lama and seat of the Tibetan government. It also contains the tombs of several previous Dalai Lamas. Richardson took this photograph during the 'Golden Procession' when, on the 30th day of the ceremonial year, sacred objects were taken from the Potala and paraded around the pilgrimage routes of Lhasa. The great Regent Sangye Gyatso (1653–1705) started this festival in commemoration of a vision seen by the 5th Dalai Lama. After the procession the great banner, or Köku ('The Silk Image'), is hauled up, covering the lower face of the palace. It is approximately 75 by 40 feet in size and consists of two panels with a huge figure of the Buddha surrounded by deities and bodhisattvas.
PRM 2001.59.8.94.1.

By their very nature photographs are, therefore, of the past. They speak to the previous existence of something, hence their intrinsic historical nature. Yet this is not an unproblematic window on the world, rather it is a 'certain but fugitive testimony'.[8] Photographs transport a past in its apparent entirety to the present and into different places. But while being 'of' space and time, they also defy space and time. In Barthes' famous phrase – the 'there-then' becomes the 'here-now'.[9] It is this 'reality effect' and immediacy of photographs that beguiles us.

Further, in a sense, photographs actually create events through their fragmenting qualities. By stilling the moment and containing it within frame, they shift experience, privileging some moments by bringing them to our attention, almost randomly, while others disappear into the mass of the unrecorded. Yet we are made conscious of the latter because of the surviving photographic fragments. Photographs create micro-events, little theatres of the moment which destabilise the broader historical narrative.[10] Yet all are linked to two agendas, 'the double desire of history', the assembling of detailed objective records and the 'restoration of a lived reality'.[11]

However, as I have suggested, for all the 'indexicality' and optical precision of photographs, they do not guarantee documentary neutrality.[12] In many ways, as a form of historical evidence, photographs are always on the line – too fragmentary, too subjective, too raw, too objectifying, too lacking in the broader term, yet too randomly inclusive.[13] Not only does the photographer select and frame his image to accord with his or her cultural vision, the first cultural editing, but the photographs themselves are infinitely recodable. Their possibilities are so various that form and content cannot necessarily be conflated with meaning. For while content can be seen as a series of signifiers, these are by no means fixed. The meanings of photographs are fluid, dependent on the knowledge viewers bring to them in a given context of viewing, inflected through different cultural ways of seeing. Looking at the same photographs, the 'truth' of Tibet will be very different to a Tibetan monk from Dharamsala than to a member of the British public seeing the same photograph in a museum.

Thinking with photographs requires a combination of macro-analytical framework with a micro-analytical methodology.[14] It has, of course, become a clichéd truism to say that photographs can only be understood in context. But context is not merely the 'who, what, why, when and where' of a photograph but the whole cultural stage,

made up of the complexities, ambiguities, serendipities and fluid relationships from which the possibility of making that photograph in that particular way emerged. So rather than endowing photographs with an unproblematic, contained meaning, context can open up the potential of photographs to other histories embedded within them.[15] Rather then, our ascription of context might also be seen as the first step in an interpretive process, placing photographs in certain relationships which engender certain meanings and ascribing the epithet of 'importance' or 'significance' accordingly. In doing this we are ascribing elements which give the photographs the kind of meanings we imagine they should give, holding them in a discourse of our own making. Thus it is inevitable that we make photographs 'mean' for us and our own particular cultural and disciplinary proclivities. This relationship is endlessly entangled, nonetheless, we can be aware of the way in which our approaches are circumscribed.

And there is a very real methodological danger in failing to do this, for over-determined concepts of 'context' can obscure readings 'against the grain' (to use Walter Benjamin's famous phrase) and obliterate the space from which other readings of the photographs and other histories might emerge in unimagined ways. Thus while the informational value of a photograph is fixed – 'this is a photograph of the Potala', its evidential value – what it actually tells people, is not.[16] As Bishop has argued, even that straightforward view of the Potala, which perhaps stands at the 'imaginal centre' of the concept of

Tibetan Doctor Reciting Religious Texts
Frederick Spencer Chapman, 1936–1937

An amchi *(Tibetan doctor) reading religious texts outside a sick man's tent. Tibetan doctors both administer herbal medicines and chant appropriate religious texts in an attempt to cure the sick. In this case, the patient may well have first been treated by Dr. William Morgan, the 1936 Mission doctor, as he is recuperating in a British military-style tent. Many Tibetans only resorted to Western medicine when all other options had been exhausted. However, surgery for conditions such as cataracts was increasingly requested by Tibetans, including monks.*
PRM 1998.131.285 .

'Lhasa' if not 'Tibet', can generate as many meanings as there are viewers, and what it stands for changes '... hover[ing] between a passing world of fantasy and romance and a sober future of science and harsh reality'.[17] As Bishop goes on, the Potala is a 'symbol of old Tibet of what has been lost, a *memento mori*', belonging to a whole twentieth century rhetoric of loss that encompasses Auschwitz to the Amazon Rain Forest.[18] The nature of photography is key to this discourse. Photographs, with their relentless pastness, yet timelessness, face us with what was, and what is in our imaginations.[19] Photographs make the past as certain as the present and can stand for that present in the way that no writing can.[20] But despite the evidential force of photographs, it remains – it can be argued – an imagined and constructed past.

Visual Economies

Of course this process of generating meanings is not random. As I have already suggested, the way subjects are represented can suggest meanings (hence the stereotype) just as can the contexts in which images are presented, both in the spaces of viewing and the material forms in which they circulate. Indeed, the processes by which we attribute meanings are almost always exclusively premised entirely on image content; seldom are the basic questions asked concerning 'the physical form, internal articulation, purpose or intellectual result' of photographs,[21] a point to which I shall return.

Poole has described the social process through which photographs acquire meaning as a 'visual economy'.[22] This might be defined as the political, social and economic matrices in which photographs operate and which pattern their production, circulation, consumption and possession. It encompasses both the production and consumption of images in a seamless flow. In this model, the social functions of the photograph are as important as the image content, but at the same time those matrices make certain kinds of images thinkable in the first place. If we are really to use photographs to think through historical relations, these elements which embed photographs are as important as the content of the photograph. In this context, it would be a mistake to think in terms of the uniqueness of images. The negative is perhaps the primary document. It is the negative which captures the light reflected off an object, passing through the aperture of a camera to be held and stilled on light sensitive chemicals spread across a support of glass or film. While the moment of inscription or exposure on the negative carries with it the authenticity of the moment, the sense of meaning created through the use of photographs emerges from the moment those negatives are first printed. What is important in the visual economy model is that photographs circulate as 'multiple originals'. That is, that all prints swapped and collected, refer back, by their very nature to the same negative, the moment of exposure. Yet although they carry the same information, their meanings differ in different performances of the image. These differences are simultaneously cohered at a broader level, precisely because of those social, political and economic elements which constitute the visual economy.

Consequently, an equally important element of the visual economy is the ownership of photographs as material objects. Who collects what? What do they do with them? How are the kept? Who sees them and who doesn't? This social process of circulation plays a major part in the formation of 'interpretative communities' premised on the exchange and cohesion of visual information within the group. Such interpretative groups make up a broader 'imagined community' – that is one which, although physically dispersed, is cohered by the sharing and exchange of symbolic values.[23] Such a circulation means that certain images accrue value,[24] greater evidential expectation being placed upon them. These processes link photographs not to an historical reality, but to an 'historical poetics' – a 'vast and sprawling domain which extends from historiography proper, through historical novels to visual art, spectacle and the historical museum'.[25]

Photographs as Objects

Thinking in terms of multiple originals leads us to a consideration of photographs not simply as images, but as images which happen to be objects. Indeed, Nuno Porto has argued that we should think of representational, imprinted objects rather than imprinted representation: 'they are made, used, kept and stored for specific reasons which do not necessarily coincide ... they can be transported, relocated, dispersed or damaged, torn and cropped ... because viewing implies one or several physical interactions'.[26] It is the material qualities which translate the abstract ideas of vision and photography into photographs and cohere the meanings of those photographs in specific contexts.[27] This is admirably demonstrated by the Tibet photographs we are considering in this volume. Nepean's little

Spencer Chapman Photographing the Regent's Procession
Evan Nepean, 1936

Spencer Chapman spent much of his time in Lhasa recording ceremonial events and processions such as this one when Reting Rinpoche, the Regent of Tibet, returned to Lhasa from a tax collecting trip. Spencer Chapman noted that, 'Gould … and Norbhu took their places in the procession while Nepean and I accompanied them to take photographs. We took several clerks and half-a-dozen scarlet-coated retainers to compete with the Chinese who would also be there. In the eyes of the Tibetans these things are of considerable importance: an official has many servants and wears as sumptuous clothes as his rank and means will allow.' (1938:217)
PRM 2001.35.176.1.

contact prints for private use, the narrative they construct in his private album and the multiple originals given to his family[28] are transformed and translated when enlarged, printed on different paper and inserted amongst Spencer Chapman's photographs in one of the official albums entitled 'Lhasa 1936', which belonged to Hugh Richardson.[29] They exhibit yet another affective tone when included in the drafts of the official albums, which constructed the 'formal and official' visual narrative. While some photographs are, in terms of images, identical, their histories, linked through sharing a 'parent' in the negative, they are all engaged with in profoundly different ways.

To give another example, the prints and lantern slides made by Tibet photographers such as Sir Charles Bell or Hugh Richardson, or those made by Spencer Chapman for his public lectures, reflect their intentions for their images. How and why were choices made? Prints made later, by institutions and researchers form another layer, they constitute an attribution of significance and interpretations to a body of material. It is through these practices that certain images become signature images of people or place. The view of the Potala from the west is a perfect example, a view produced by almost every photographer who has photographed in Tibet and reproduced in almost every book on Tibet, it speaks to the authenticity of observation by placing the photographer within easily recognised spatial relations with the icon of 'Tibet'.[30] Such repetition of images cannot be seen in terms of duplication but, as I have argued, multiple originals because they were all made within a specific historical moment for a specific reason. The material forms in which the photographs are presented becomes integral to their meaning. To ignore these elements is to miss much of the historical evidence that photographs provide, for by their nature they are constantly active in the present.

In the Museum

This places a particular duty on institutions which care for photographs that might function cross-culturally and inscribe multiple and perhaps competing or contested histories.[31] Thus, the contexts we apply to a photograph in the process of, for instance, cataloguing and describing cannot be seen as neutral practices. It is the acute awareness of these cultural practices which underlies the curatorial practices in relation to photographs at the Pitt Rivers Museum, the guiding principles of our thinking. This, obviously, cannot be separated from the research process as the exhibition, 'Seeing Lhasa' amply demonstrates. The exhibition would not have been possible in this particular form and narrative without the critical curatorial practices which move beyond image content and enmesh the photographs. Likewise, those curatorial practices can only exist in a symbiotic and inseparable relationship with research.

For instance, how would our understanding of the visualisation of Tibet in the mid-twentieth century be changed if, curatorially, it had been said of Bell's copy negatives of Martin's photographs from the early twentieth century,[32] that they were 'only' copies, and either destroyed or relegated to an uncatalogued box of 'duplicates' in the attic? This we might characterise as a conventional 'art historical' model of curatorship which privileges singularity and the status of the maker. Conversely, the 'picture library' mentality is too often concerned only with the forensics of image, regardless of the specific historicity of the photograph's materiality. This has meant that photographs have been 'archived' with little concern for the historical objects themselves. Not only have photographs been torn from albums, removed from

original mounts and captions, but format changes – such as copy prints which have cropped the image – have remained unrecorded. Such practices have resulted in ' a massive dehistorcization and decontextualization which, if it had occurred with documents, would create a massive scandal'.[33]

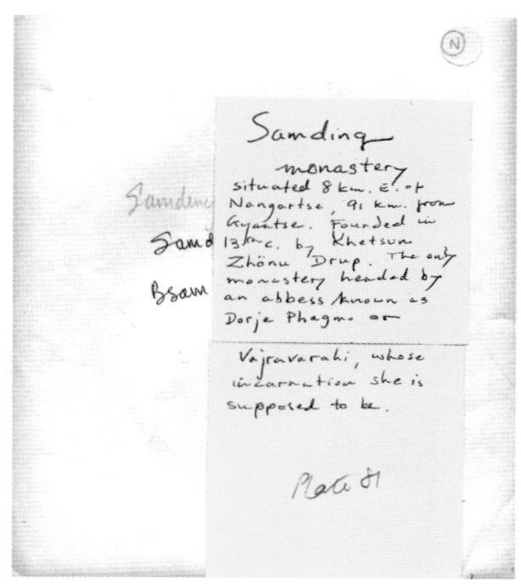

Re-photographed View of Samding Monastery
Hugh Richardson, c. 1936–1950

Samding monastery (south of Lhasa) was founded in the 13th century and is the only Tibetan monastery headed by a woman, known as Dorje Phagmo. Richardson has re-photographed this picture of Samding against a wooden surface. The reverse carries annotations in Richardson's handwriting and a label giving further information about the monastery has been added by someone else.
PRM 2001.59.2.80.2.

Layers of captions, for instance, indicate not perhaps misinformation or incorrect information to be superseded by 'correct captions', but are part of a history of how an image was perceived, identified, understood and articulated at a given moment in its history. Such information must be recorded for the caption, in either the museum or publication, becomes an important instrument of 'refined and inter-connected narratives marking out parameters of meaning'.[34] Thus we can argue that the history of collecting and description of an image is vital to how we might understand the constructions of Tibet as images themselves. This cannot be separated out from, for instance, aesthetics, but exists in a mutually sustaining relationship of significance.

In the new digitally dominated world, these problems are multiplied as photographs are chosen for digitalisation and web dissemination for reasons of aesthetic, and thus commercial, appeal, rather than for their historical importance. They are reduced to a consistency of style and shape for attractive viewing on a computer screen. Photographs become sad 'digital orphans', separated from their materiality, their context and ultimately, history.[35] It is precisely this tendency that we intend to counter in the Pitt Rivers Museum's forthcoming *Tibetan Visual History On-line 1920–1950*,[36] which will also attend to the performances of images in different contexts and in different formats, adhering to the principles of research-led curatorship which I outlined above.

Conclusion

Photographs are amongst the most potent of 'Tibetan' museum objects. They have an enormous and twofold potential. They are an evidential source for Tibetan communities wherever they might be and whomever they might be, inscribing complex layers of cultural information and knowledge, constituted continually through different moments of the photographs' existence. As Western-produced objects, the photographs are equally evidential sources of the Western cultures with whom Tibetan experience intersected. But as I have suggested, they are more than simply 'pictures of things'. Photographs are historical objects to think with to the fullest extent that this implies. To engage with this potential has major implications not only for museums, such as the Pitt Rivers, holding collections of photographs, but the whole process of understanding the past through these wonderful, compelling, dynamic and volatile documents which have the potential to unlock histories in ways previously unimaginable.

Notes

1. Berger 1980:55
2. Schwartz 1995:42.
3. There is a massive theoretical literature on this, see for instance Barthes (1977, 1984), Kracauer (1980, 1995), Benjamin (1973) and more recently Burgin (1982), Tagg (1988), Metz (1985) and Maynard (1997), to name but a few.
4. It is, of course, this analogical certainty of the link between the photograph and the physical world which has been irrevocably severed by digital technologies.
5. Tagg 1995:286.
6. Barthes 1984:87, 107.
7. This has been so since the advent of the negative/positive process in the 1840s. There are, of course, some technologies where this does not apply, for instance daguerreotypes or polaroids.
8. Barthes 1984:87, 107.
9. Barthes 1977:44.

10. I have discussed the performative element of photographs as historical sources in Edwards 2001a: 16–21; 2001b.
11. Tagg 1995:290.
12. Schwartz 1995:44.
13. Edwards 2001a:8–13 2001b.17.
14. Schwartz 1995:42.
15. I have explored these ideas in detail in relation to two photographs from Samoa. See Edwards (2001a:107–110).
16. Schwartz 1995:51.
17. Bishop 1994:13.
18. Bishop 1994:17.
19. There is a substantial and growing literature on photography, memory and loss, much of it generated in Holocaust studies, see for example Rabinowitz (1994), Kuhn (1995), Van Alphen (1997) and Langford (2001).
20. Tagg 1995:296.
21. Schwartz 1995:44.
22. Poole 1997:9–13.
23. Anderson 1983.
24. Poole 1997:11.
25. Bann 1984:3–4.
26. Porto 2001:38
27. Edwards 2002
28. I am grateful to Judy Goldthorp for explaining the relationship between these different objects. Identical albums containing the same photographs were made up, and although they were all captioned in different hands, this was done under Nepean's guidance.
29. Now in the Department of Oriental Antiquities, British Museum (No. 1986.3.13).
30. Bishop 1997.
31. See Edwards 2001a:108–110.
32. Bell made glass plate copies of Henry Martin's negatives of 1908–14 and absorbed them into his own visual archive on Tibet, documenting them along with his own photographs.
33. Hayes et al 1998:6.
34. Tagg 1995:293.
35. Sassoon, forthcoming.
36. This project is beginning developed in collaboration with the British Museum.

Tibetan Photographic Collections at The Pitt Rivers Museum

Charles Alfred Bell (1870–1945)

Charles Alfred Bell was born in Calcutta, India, on 31 October 1870 – the son of Henry Bell of the Indian Civil Service (ICS). Educated in Winchester and New College, Oxford, Charles also joined the ICS in 1891 and spent the next nine years in various posts in Bengal, Bihar and Orissa, before being transferred to Darjeeling in 1900. It was here that he had his first contact with Tibetans and became fascinated with the people and their culture.

Bell at once applied himself to learning the Tibetan language. This led to the publication, in 1905, of his first book, *A Manual of Colloquial Tibetan*, a two-part grammar-phrase book and dictionary. During the next few years Bell became increasingly involved in the political affairs of Tibet and the surrounding regions. In 1904–1905 he was put in charge of the administration of the Chumbi valley area, which had been temporarily ceded by Tibet to Britain under the terms of the Younghusband Treaty. Bell also served time as the acting Political Officer for Sikkim, Bhutan and Tibet during the absence of John C. White, before succeeding him in the post in 1908.

The most significant event during Bell's time as Political Officer was meeting the 13th Dalai Lama in 1910. His Holiness was forced to flee Tibet, seeking refuge in Sikkim, when Chinese invaders entered Lhasa. As Political Officer, it was Bell who was put in charge of dealing with the Dalai Lama. The two formed an intimate and lasting friendship, which was to prove critical to the British in their future negotiations and dealings with Tibet after the Dalai Lama's return to Lhasa in June 1912. Through their personal relationship, Bell and the Dalai Lama helped to build trust and understanding between the two nations. As Bell himself stated, the assistance given to the Dalai Lama during his exile was 'perhaps the chief reason why the British name stands high in Tibet' (Bell 1924: 111).

Bell's Tibetan acumen was next put to use during the British treaty negotiations with the Tibetans in 1913–1914. Bell played an important role in these negotiations as advisor on Tibetan affairs to the British plenipotentiary, Sir Henry McMahon. A treaty was signed which set out new Anglo-Tibetan

Sir Charles Bell, the Maharajah of Sikkim and the 13th Dalai Lama

A Gelukpa Monk (opposite)
Sir Charles Bell (or Rabden), *c.* 1920

An unidentified Gelukpa monk with the implements used in his religious practice including a bell, dorje, *skull cup and drum. Bell's notes on this image state: 'In the skull cup is tea without anything, e.g. butter etc., added to it. This he offers to the gods. In the bowl on the left are fruits which he eats. The staff at the side he uses when walking. It has a ring round it which he shakes when he reaches his destination, and, hearing this, people bring him food, so that he does not have to ask for it.'*
PRM BL.H.195A.

trade regulations. That Tibetans agreed to the deal was very much a reflection of the confidence that the Dalai Lama and his representative, Prime Minister (Lönchen) Shatra, had in Bell. For his part in the negotiations Bell was awarded a CMG (knighthood).

Bell continued as Political Officer for Sikkim, Bhutan and Tibet until 1918. During this time he continued his communications with the Dalai Lama who introduced many modernisations into Tibet, often acting upon Bell's advice. Bell was widely acknowledged as the authority on Tibetan matters at the time.

After 1918 Bell took leave from the Civil Service and devoted himself to the study of Tibet, spending the next two years in Darjeeling. Although he had, for many years, an open invitation from the Dalai Lama to visit Lhasa, a British Government agreement did not allow him to do so. In 1919 however, this situation changed and when the then Political Officer, Captain W.L. Campbell, resigned unexpectedly, Bell took up the position again – on the understanding that there was a strong possibility that he would be allowed to visit Lhasa. He was finally given government permission to visit the Tibetan capital as part of a diplomatic mission in 1920, arriving in the city on 17 November. Bell's role was to advise Tibet on foreign policy. 'The Dalai Lama showed his more than friendly intentions by receiving Sir Bell, at the very first interview, informally, sitting with him at a small table in his private apartment, with no witness present. This was regarded by the people of Lhasa as a special honour, as it was the custom for His Holiness to receive even the highest Tibetan officials while seated on his dais.' (Spencer Chapman 1938:144)

Bell remained in Lhasa for the best part of a year. After his return, in 1921, he left the ICS and applied himself to writing about Tibet. In his retirement, Bell published several books on Tibetan culture and history – *Tibet: Past and Present* in 1920, followed by *The People of Tibet* in 1928, and *The Religion of Tibet* in 1931. He also continued his personal correspondence with the Dalai Lama. In 1934 Bell returned to Tibet, with his wife. Unfortunately he was too late to meet his old friend again, for the 13th Dalai Lama had passed away in December 1933. Bell continued his travels in Central Asia during the next few years visiting Mongolia, Manchuria and Siberia.

Fittingly, Bell's final work was a result of the strong bond that he had formed with the 13th Dalai Lama since their first meeting in 1910. The book, *Portrait of the Dalai Lama*, was completed only a few days before Bell's death in Canada (to where he had recently emmigrated) on 8 March 1945.

Sir Charles Bell was probably the most influential British officer to serve in Tibet. He set the groundwork for Anglo-Tibetan relations, and his Mission opened the way for subsequent British officials to visit Lhasa. Bell's strength lay in his ability to immerse himself in Tibetan culture and language, becoming, in his own words, 'in a large measure Tibetanised' (Bell 1946:29). This earned him the respect and acceptance of the local people. As one Tibetan official said, 'When a European is with us Tibetans I feel that he is a European and we are Tibetans; but when Lonchen Bell is with us, I feel that we are all Tibetans together.' (Bell 1924:206)

Bell Collection

The Pitt Rivers Museum (PRM), University of Oxford, holds a collection of approximately 800 photographs belonging to Charles Bell (accession numbers 1998.285.1–1998.285.505 [BL.H, BL.P, BL.Q]). These are all original glass plate negatives. For research and handling purposes, the Museum has a set of contact prints made from these negatives. The Bell collection was donated to the PRM by St. Antony's College in 1983. It was previously held at the Royal Central Asiatic Society.

The Bell collection is organised, following Bell's own numbering system, into three main series, 'H' (half-plate),'P' (postcard size) and 'Q' (quarter-plate). The Museum also has a copy of Bell's own handlist that gives full descriptions and details about each image. The collection includes, not only photographs taken by Charles Bell, but images collected by him from other photographers (including Henry Martin and David Macdonald). Most of these images were accumulated by Bell for use as illustrations in his books.

His photographs were taken mainly during his Mission to Lhasa in 1920–1921. However, there are a number of earlier images dating as far back as 1903. While the majority were taken in Tibet, there were also approximately 80 taken in India (particularly in Sikkim where Bell was stationed as the Political Officer), as well as a few from Nepal and Bhutan. Not surprisingly, the areas of Tibet photographed by Bell are on the main trade route between India and Lhasa through the Chumbi valley, although the majority of his photographs were taken in Lhasa itself.

Bell's photographs are generally acknowledged as being well composed and illustrating a good photographic eye. He used a traditional plate and tripod camera with glass negatives. A number of Bell's photographs were actually taken by his Sikkimese orderly, Rabden Lepcha, as Bell acknowledged in the handlist he compiled '[he] was with me for 18 years and took many of my photos for me.'

The collection is diverse in its subject matter and contains portraits, architecture, natural history and landscapes. It also includes several portraits of the 13th Dalai Lama. These were taken, at the Dalai Lama's request, both in Calcutta in 1910 during His Holiness' exile, and in the Tibetan capital. Bell was also fortunate to be able to photograph many important ceremonies and events in Lhasa, including New Year Festival celebrations such as the *Mönlam Chenmo* (Great Prayer Festival) and the *Dzong Gyap Shambe* – a gun and arrow shooting competition. Although Bell was able to have access to some of the most important people and holiest places in Tibet, he was also interested in everyday life in the Tibetan capital. He photographed people from all levels of society including officials and government delegations, abbots and monks, herdsmen and traders, and soldiers, convicts and beggars. Similarly, Bell's photographs not only include images of palaces and monasteries but also of streets, houses, schools and markets. In this way Bell's photographs offer an insight into the daily lives of Tibetans.

The Pitt Rivers Museum also holds a small number of Charles Bell's manuscripts. These include several diaries from his 1933–1935 travels to Tibet, Mongolia and Russia, and general notes on Tibetan life and his career in the Indian Civil Service.

Claire Freeman

Frederick Spencer Chapman (1907–1971)

Spencer Chapman with Ciné Camera in Tibet
Evan Nepean, 1936
PRM 2001.35.213.1.

Frederick Spencer Chapman was born in London on 10 May 1907. His mother, Winifred Ormond, died shortly after his birth and his father, Frank Spencer Chapman, was killed at the battle of the Somme. Freddy (as he was to become known) and his older brother, Robert, were cared for by an elderly clergyman and his wife. Freddy developed an early interest in nature and the outdoors. As a boy he was, by his own account, 'first a mad-keen butterfly collector, then a wild-flower enthusiast, and at last a bird-watcher' (Spencer Chapman 1953: 23). This was a continuing interest throughout his school years and into his adult life.

Chapman was educated at Sedbergh School in Cumbria and then won a Kitchener scholarship to St. John's College, Cambridge, studying history and English. It was here that he developed his passion for adventure and, by the end of his university years, he had already completed several overseas excursions including a climbing expedition in the Alps and a journey to Iceland to study the plant and bird life.

After finishing university Chapman spent several years in Greenland (1930–1931 and 1932–1933) as part of two expedition parties investigating possible air routes between Europe and America. Chapman undertook surveying work and was also hired as a ski expert and ornithologist. He had already shown a flair for photography and was told before he left to, '... try and get really good at mountain photography if you have got a camera ...' (Barker 1975: 73). Upon his return from the Arctic, Chapman produced the film 'Northern Lights' and wrote the official account of each of the expeditions which were published as *Northern Lights* (1932) and *Watkins' Last Expedition* (1934). As he was a talented speaker, Chapman was soon giving lectures about his adventures in the Arctic also. Throughout the rest of his career he was often in demand in this capacity and his life provided him with no shortage of material based on his standard topics of exploration and danger. Chapman next turned his hand to teaching, accepting a post at Aysgarth Preparatory School in Yorkshire, where he found satisfaction in being able to pass his own love of nature and the outdoor life on to many of his pupils. However, his passion for adventure was far from sated and, early in 1936, he joined a Himalayan climbing expedition. It was during this trip that he first met Basil Gould, the Political Officer for Sikkim, who offered him a job as his private secretary for the 1936–1937 Diplomatic Mission to Lhasa, Tibet.

The Mission to Lhasa departed from Gangtok (Sikkim) in late July 1936 and they left Tibet just over six months later in February 1937. The aim of the mission was to advise the Regent and his Cabinet, to persuade the Panchen Lama to return from China where he had fled, and, if possible, to establish permanent British representation in Lhasa. The Mission personnel, under the leadership of Gould, included Hugh Richardson, the British Trade Agent at Gyantse, and Lieutenant Evan Nepean, one of two telegraph operators sent from the Royal Signal Corps.

Chapman's main role in the Mission was to decipher telegraphs, but in reality he did much more than this. 'I have to take film and still photos, do bird, plant and bug work, some survey, and personal work for Gould ...' (Barker 1975:131) He was also responsible for keeping the *Mission Diary*, which was accompanied by photographs and sent off to the Government of India each week and spent his spare time bird-watching (an interest shared with Richardson) and hill-climbing. Chapman was also a major exponent of the British Mission's entertainment programme. He spent many hours editing and sorting ciné film for showing to the Tibetans and was one of the keenest players in the 'Mission Marmots' football team. It was due in part to these events that the Mission was able to make a good impression on the locals and it was considered that Chapman's 'open, cheerful friendliness went down well with the Tibetans' (Barker 1975:135).

In 1937, after his return from Lhasa, Chapman secured permission to lead a small climbing expedition to the Tibetan holy mountain, Chomolhari. Chapman and a sherpa, Passang Dawa, succeeded in becoming the first mountaineers to reach the 24,000 foot summit. Tibet also provided Chapman with material for two new books – *Lhasa: The Holy City* (1938) and *Helvellyn to Himalaya* (1940).

In 1938, Chapman returned to teaching, taking an appointment at Gordonstoun School in the north of Scotland. However, war was on the horizon and Chapman was soon called up for active service. He held a number of short-term posts before he was dispatched, in September 1941, to command a guerrilla warfare school in Singapore. Chapman was soon sent behind the Japanese lines to organise reconnaissance and sabotage operations. He excelled in this role, spending three and a half years (1942–1945) in the Malayan jungle. By the end of the war he was justifiably labelled a hero, promoted to Lieutenant-Colonel, and awarded a DSO in 1944 and bar in 1946. His story of these years was published in his enormously successful 1948 book, *The Jungle is Neutral.*

After the war, Chapman married Faith Mary Townson and became the First Organising Secretary (Director) of the Outward Bound Trust. He then returned again to teaching: as headmaster of the British Forces' King Alfred School in Plön, West Germany (1948–1952) and then at St. Andrew's College, Grahamstown, South Africa (1956–1961) and later as warden for the Pestalozzi Children's Village for displaced children in Sedlescombe, Sussex (1962–1966). In between he still made time for another adventure – caravanning from Cape Town to Uganda with his wife and three small boys in 1953. *Lightest Africa*, an account of this trip, was published in 1955.

Chapman spent his last years working as the warden of Wantage Hall (a student hall of residence) at Reading University. However, as retirement approached, he felt under increasing pressure from health and financial worries. Also, despite leading such an extraordinary life, Chapman still felt unfulfilled. For someone who had always sought 'to experience the fullness of life, and the inner satisfaction that comes from facing and overcoming danger', (Chapman 1953:16) old age offered no redemption. Frederick Spencer Chapman shot himself on 8 August 1971.

Chapman's medals and awards include: Arctic Medal (1931), Gill Memorial Medal (Royal Geographical Society, 1941), Mungo Park Medal (Royal Scottish Geographical Society, 1948), Sunday Times Special Award and Gold Medal (1949) and the Lawrence of Arabia Memorial Medal (Royal Central Asian Society, 1950). He was also the subject of 'This is Your Life' on 23 December 1963.

Spencer Chapman Collection

The Pitt Rivers Museum (PRM) holds a large collection of Frederick Spencer Chapman's photographs. This totals about 2,500 images including not only Chapman's Tibet photographs, but also many taken during his other expeditions and travels. Chapman's wife, Faith Spencer Chapman, donated the collection to the PRM in 1994.

There are about 900 photographs taken by Chapman during the Diplomatic Mission to Lhasa in 1936–1937. These include a series of 98 Dufaycolour transparencies (accession numbers 1998.157.1–98 [SC.T.1–98]), examples of one of the earliest uses of colour film. Most of the other images (accession numbers 1998.131.1–708 [SC.T.2] and 1998.132.1–6 [SC.T.3]) come in various, sometimes multiple, formats: mostly as prints (nearly 400), some as negatives (over 100), as well as nearly 100 lantern slides. In addition to Tibet, this series includes images from India, either at the Gangtok residency or on the road into Tibet. There are also some photographs of the two climbing expeditions that Chapman undertook before and after the Tibet Mission (to the Zemu Glacier in 1936 and to Chomolhari in 1937).

Lhasa: The Holy City, Chapman's 1938 account of the Mission to Tibet, provides a lot of information about the photographs that he took and about his photographic tools. Chapman was equipped in Tibet with five still cameras (three Zeiss and two Contax), one of which was loaded with colour film, and four ciné cameras: a 35mm camera with tripod and three 16mm cine cameras. Not surprisingly Chapman writes of the trek into Tibet that, 'some difficulty was experienced in carrying my cameras ... I packed most of the cameras in a large rucksack which was carried, not without some complaint, by one of the grooms' (Spencer Chapman 1938:18). As Chapman often wanted to use 'all this formidable battery of cameras more or less at the same time' (Spencer Chapman 1938:246), he often worked with Lieutenant Nepean recording events with both still and moving images.

Chapman took a range of images in Tibet. In a way his photographs mirror those of Charles Bell who, 16 years before him, travelled the same route from Gangtok to Lhasa photographing the main sites on the way such as Phari, Gyantse, Yamdrok Tso and, of course, the Potala. Like Bell, Chapman's official status meant that he had access to the top levels of society. For example, he was able to take photographs and take cinema film of the Regent and of various Shapés (cabinet ministers), magistrates and lay officials. Chapman's other portraits are more eclectic in nature and include outcasts, traders, children, nomads and the military. It is also worth noting that in the Spencer Chapman collection there are a number of photographs of both the 13th and 14th Dalai Lama. Chapman must have acquired rather than taken these photographs however – he only arrived in Lhasa after the death of the 13th Dalai Lama and left before the 14th incarnation was identified.

The Mission were also invited to view, either as official guests or as spectators, many ceremonial processions and festivals as 'the Tibetan officials and people ... were anxious that we, as their guests, should be given full opportunity to witness these scenes' (Spencer Chapman 1938:216). These included the major celebrations for the Tibetan New Year (such as the *Namdrogatse* – New Year Sky Dancing Rope Game and the *Dzong Gyap Shambe* – archery competition), and the Regent's tour to and from Samye monastery, all of which Chapman was able to photograph.

As well as the Tibetan material, Chapman's collection includes photographs taken in Lapland, from his two expeditions to Greenland (1930–1933), and a series taken during a trip in SE Asia (accession numbers: 1998.133–1998.156 [SC.A]). Chapman also took ciné film footage during most of his trips and the PRM was the recipient of many of these films, including two reels shot in Tibet (in both colour and black and white) as well as footage of Greenland, Lapland and Africa.

The Museum's manuscript collections have some of Chapman's diaries – those of his second trip to Greenland in 1934, to the Alps in 1935, and four diaries spanning his time in Malaya during the war (1944–1945) – and various miscellaneous notes made for public lectures. In addition, the Museum also has a gilded brass statue that was collected by Chapman toward the end of the Lhasa expedition and donated by his wife in 1994.

Claire Freeman

Hugh Richardson in Lhasa
Frederick Spencer Chapman,
1936–1937
PRM 1998.131.669.

Hugh Edward Richardson (1905–2000)

Hugh Edward Richardson was born in St. Andrews, Scotland on 22 December 1905. He was the son of Colonel Hugh Richardson, a military doctor and university lecturer, and grandson of an Indian Civil Service officer. Richardson was educated at Salvator's School, St Andrews, and Trinity College, Glenalmond, and went on to study classics at Keble College, Oxford.

After a brief stint teaching at his old school in Glenalmond, Richardson followed his grandfather's footsteps and joined the Indian Civil Service in 1930. He was stationed in Bengal as Sub-Divisional Officer from 1932 to 1934. It was during this time that Richardson first became interested in Tibet – learning the language from a Tibetan servant, and travelling through Sikkim and into Tibet as far as Phari, during leave in 1933. This first encounter with Tibet was the beginning of a lifelong interest in the land and its people.

In 1934, Richardson was appointed to Loralai, Baluchistan (Pakistan) as Assistant Political Agent where he served under Basil Gould. Gould was impressed by Richardson and knew of his interest in Tibet and so, when Gould took up the position of Political Agent for Sikkim, Bhutan and Tibet in 1935, he helped Richardson to secure a posting in Tibet. So it was that in July 1936 Richardson took up the appointment of Trade Agent at Gyantse and was called upon to be a part of the Political Mission to Lhasa, which was mounted at the same time.

The Political Mission arrived in Lhasa in August 1936. The eight-man delegation was under the leadership of Basil Gould, and amongst Richardson's companions in the party were Frederick Spencer Chapman and Evan Nepean. Richardson's role in the Mission was to open communications with the Tibetan government officials and to work with Gould in developing Tibetan-British policy. The Mission remained in Lhasa for six months. Officially, their role was to mediate for the return of the Panchen (Tashi) Lama from exile in China. Unofficially, however, the Mission was mounted to counter the presence of Chinese officials in the Tibetan capital. It was agreed that the British should maintain a permanent presence in Lhasa. Therefore, after Gould and the bulk of the party left Lhasa in February 1937, Richardson remained behind as the first Head of the British Mission in Lhasa. In this capacity, Richardson spent a total of eight years resident in Tibet – from 1936–1940 and 1947–1950.

During the years he was living in Lhasa, Richardson was able to become fluent in the Tibetan language and familiar with the country and its people. He made friends with many of Tibet's leading officials including the young 14th Dalai Lama. Although protocol did not allow Richardson to meet the Tibetan leader in private, he was able to communicate with him through the Austrian refugees, Heinrich Harrer and Peter Aufschnaiter, sending messages and gifts. Richardson had to wait until the Dalai Lama fled Tibet for India in 1959 to meet him in private. Richardson established friendships with Tibetans of all classes gaining their respect through his appreciation of Tibetan culture and affection for its people.

The relative peace and stability of Tibet at the time Richardson was there allowed him to travel widely. He saw much of Central Tibet, visiting all the major monasteries, and often going out of his way to see historical inscriptions on pillars. The study of these ancient inscribed pillars (*doring*) was one of Richardson's enduring scholarly interests. As a permanent resident in Lhasa, Richardson was also able to witness many important Tibetan ceremonies. As he stated in his book, *Ceremonies of the Lhasa Year*, 'when one was accepted by the officials of the Tibetan Government they always seemed eager that their guests should attend the ceremonies. They arranged seating with a good view but at a discreet distance ...' (Richardson 1993:8).

When he was not occupied with his official duties, Richardson had time to pursue his own interests. His hobbies were ornithology, botany and gardening, and he was also an enthusiastic photographer. Another of Richardson's passions was golf, which he introduced to the Tibetans, although the ball tended to travel 'rather too far in the thin air' (Croston 2001).

Richardson did not remain in Tibet during the war years. However, before he left in 1939, he witnessed the arrival in Lhasa of the recently 'discovered' 14th incarnation of the Dalai Lama and was able to take many photographs of the procession into the city. Unfortunately Richardson was then posted to India and so was not able to attend the Installation ceremony in February 1940. During his time away from Tibet, Richardson held several appointments in Pakistan, China and India. He returned to Lhasa in 1946 to resume his post as Officer-in-Charge of the British Mission. After India gained its independence from Britain in 1947, he continued in the post as the Indian Government representative. In doing so he was probably the last British official to occupy an important Indian diplomatic posting. He made an OBE in 1944 and a Companion of the Indian Empire (CIE) in 1947.

In August 1950, only a few months before the Chinese invasion of Tibet, Richardson left the civil service and Lhasa. He had been aware of the changing politics of the time and the growing threat from China. Richardson spent a short time in Malaya before retiring to St Andrews, where he married Huldah Rennie in 1951 (and continued to play golf as one of the longest serving members of the Royal and Ancient Golf Club).

Richardson then began a second career as a Tibetan scholar. His understanding of Tibetan culture and history was such that he became one of the finest of his era, the 'father of modern Tibetan studies'. (McKay 1997:222) He published several books and articles including: *A Cultural History of Tibet* (1986, co-authored with David Snellgrove); *Ceremonies of the Lhasa Year* (1993); and *High Peaks, Pure Earth* (1998), a collection of papers and articles edited by his friend and colleague Michael Aris. Richardson's books are decidedly academic in nature – he divulged little of his own personal thoughts and feelings. 'His writing energies went into the historical and cultural – self-revelation would have been totally out of character' (Croston 2001).

During these later years Richardson lectured in Tibetan history and language at several universities. He obtained an Honorary D. Litt from the University of St Andrews in 1985 and became an Honorary Fellow of both the British Academy (1986) and of Keble College (1981). Along with David Snellgrove, Richardson was a founder-trustee of the Institute of Tibetan Studies in Tring. Richardson also continued to maintain links with the Tibetan exile community and with the Dalai Lama. He played a major role in the founding of the Tibet Society of the UK in 1959. Up until his death, Richardson was an advocate for Tibetan independence, both in his books, such as *Tibet and its History* and *A Cultural History of Tibet*, and in the political arena. In 1950, he accompanied a delegation to New York to lobby for the United Nations to oppose the Chinese occupation of Tibet. Richardson was also critical of his own government's stance, stating that, '... the British Government, the only government among Western countries to have had treaty relations with Tibet, sold the Tibetans down the rivers and since then have constantly cold-shouldered the Tibetans so that in 1959 they would not even support a resolution in the UN condemning the violation of human rights in Tibet by the Chinese' (Richardson, Hugh, 'My Direct Experience of Independent Tibet 1936–49', Tibet Society of the UK Information Sheet, London).

Richardson died at St. Andrews on 3 December 2000, aged 94, after a long illness. His loss was felt in both this country and in Tibet – at the time of his memorial service in Scotland, butter lamps were lit in the Jo khang in Lhasa in his honour. The Dalai Lama also sent a personal letter expressing his sadness: "... I consider him not only a personal friend but also a very good friend of the Tibetan nation and its people ... And because he had lived in Tibet and known Tibet and the Tibetans intimately he was truly precious to us... With his death Tibet had lost one of its foremost champions ...' (Message from the Dalai Lama, 7 December 2000).

Richardson Collection

Hugh Richardson's photographs were donated to the Pitt Rivers Museum by his executors in 2001 (accession number 2001.59). The collection contains almost 1,800 nitrate film negatives taken by Richardson mostly during the years he spent living and travelling in Tibet and the surrounding areas (India and Bhutan) from 1930–1950. The collection also includes well over 1,000 black and white and colour prints, and transparency slides. These consist of, not only prints made from Richardson's negatives, but also prints and slides of Tibet that he was given or collected from other photographers, including some relatively modern images. Richardson's collection also includes related Tibetan visual material from other sources such as a number of commercial postcards and VHS tapes.

Because Richardson was able to travel extensively within Tibet, the locations of his photographs are wide ranging. There are many photographs of Lhasa, of the major monasteries and of sights along the main India–Tibet trade corridor, but Richardson was also able to photograph many less commonly visited locations, such as Nyemo and Drikhung and places in the Yarlung and Lhobrag valleys.

Richardson's images include many landscapes and views, as well as portraits of both high- and low-ranking Tibetans. There are also many photographs of classic Tibetan scenes such as the Potala, of which he said, 'I wasted a lot of film on the Potala – I have all these views of it' (Croston 2001). To a degree though, his photographs reflect many of his personal and academic pursuits. For example, his collection contains a vast number of photographs showing *doring* (inscribed pillars) – a particular area of interest for Richardson. Also, being a keen naturalist, a number of Richardson's photographs are of birds and other wildlife. The most distinctive feature of Richardson's photographs, however, is their scholarly – rather than purely aesthetic – focus. In particular, he took many photographs of important historical and cultural sites, including stupas and temples, religious art and edifices, as well as ceremonial events.

As Head of the British Mission, Richardson was invited to most of the important Tibetan events, both secular and religious, and his photographs provide a nearly complete visual record of the ceremonial year (many of which appear in his book, *Ceremonies of the Lhasa Year* [1993]). Amongst the celebrations that Richardson photographed are the *Mönlam Chenmo* (The Great Prayer Festival); the *Chönga Chöpa* (The Offerings of the Fifteenth) when huge frames decorated with coloured butter are displayed; the *Mönlam Torgya* (Casting out the Votive Offering for the Great Prayer); the Demon-Ransom King or Scapegoat ceremony; and the dances of the *Tse Gutor*.

Since the Chinese invasion, many of the monastic sights that Richardson saw have been destroyed and many of the cultural ceremonies are no longer performed. The words he wrote for *A Cultural History of Tibet* still ring true, 'the civilization of the Tibetan people is disappearing before our very eyes …' (Richardson and Snellgrove 1968:15). In light of this, Richardson's collection stands as a unique testimony to a culture drastically changed in the past fifty years.

Claire Freeman

Evan Yorke Nepean (1909–2002)

Evan Yorke Nepean was born in November 1909, the son of Major Sir Charles Molyneux Yorke Nepean and Mary Winifred Swayne. He was educated at Winchester and Downing College, Cambridge where he read Natural Sciences. After graduating in 1931, he joined the

Evan Nepean in Lhasa
Frederick Spencer Chapman, 1936
PRM 1998.131.445.

Royal Corps of Signals and was commissioned in 1933. He was then sent to the North West Frontier Province of India where he remained for five years. Alongside his military duties, he learnt to speak Urdu (Croston 2002b:1).

In July 1936, he was summoned to join the Mission to Lhasa headed by Basil Gould. He was joined by a fellow Signals officer, Sidney Dagg. At this time: 'A telegraph line operated as far as Lhasa. It was a single strand of galvanised iron wire supported on light wooden poles with no specific insulation ... Mounted linesmen patrolled the route re-erecting any poles that were blown down and repairing breaks in the line' (Croston 2002a:39). Nepean and Dagg's task was to set up and operate a portable wireless which could transmit messages should the Mission go beyond Lhasa. In the event, the Mission remained in Lhasa but the setting up of the wireless had a great impact in the city. It enabled the British to counter the influence of the Chinese wireless operator and curb the Chinese monopoly on supplying outside information to the Tibetan government.

Nepean spent three months in Lhasa before being recalled by his commanding officer to the North West Frontier. During his time with the Mission, he and Dagg were kept fully occupied transmitting cipher messages to the Government of India. They expertly addressed themselves to the challenge of transmitting at high altitude. Not only did they occupy themselves with official matters, but they also exchanged messages with amateurs in different parts of the world. They also made a significant contribution to an important task of the Mission, namely, strengthening and improving relations with the Tibetan government and the local populace. One way in which this was achieved was by providing Lhasa residents with entertainment in the form of film shows. It was Nepean and Dagg who had the task of setting up the equipment and working the projector at the Dekyi Lingka. Also, Nepean worked together with and assisted Spencer Chapman in taking photographs.

In 1939, Nepean was recalled to Britain to work for MI8 on codes and ciphers. In 1940, he married Georgiana Cicely Willoughby with whom he had three daughters. In 1941, he was posted to Iraq after which he joined the 8th Army in Egypt. He inherited the baronetcy from his father in 1953. In 1957, he retired from the army after post war appointments in Singapore and Germany and worked for the Civil Service. In 1959, he took a retired officer's staff appointment in the Chief Signal Officer's branch at HQ Southern Command until his retirement in 1973. He died in Salisbury, Wiltshire in March 2002.

Nepean Collection

The Nepean collection was donated to the Pitt Rivers Museum by Judy Goldthorp (née Nepean) in 2001. It comprises 94 black-and-white negatives and 391 black and white images (90 x 60 mm). They illustrate the journey made by the 1936 Gould Mission from Gangtok to Lhasa via Jelap La, Natu

La, Changdu dak bungalow, the Kargyu Gompa and Yatung. In Yatung the party was greeted by school children waving Union Jacks and the 2/7th Rajput dramatic club put on a performance. From Yatung the route took them to Gautsa, Tuna and Kala to Gyantse. Here the members of the Mission were entertained by pony and yak races. From Gyantse the route to Lhasa went via Karo La, Pede and Chaksam. In Lhasa the Mission stayed at the Dekyi Lingka. The collection includes a sequence of photographs taken by Nepean of a ritual performed by the monks at Kundeling (the monastery which owned the Dekyi Lingka) designed to ward off illness in the middle of winter. Scenes shot in the environs of Lhasa feature a visit to Sera monastery, the streets and circumambulatory path around the Barkhor area, the Snake Temple (Lukhang) and activities such as paper making, threshing and winnowing. There are also photographs of the Regent Reting's return to Lhasa (after a tax collecting trip) and shots of the review of the Tibetan army by Colonel Neame and other members of the 1936 Mission. As one of two wireless operators on the Mission, Nepean dedicates several images to the radio transmission equipment being carried by coolies, the hand-charging generator used to power the system and the equipment set up indoors in Gyantse and outside in a tent in the grounds of Dekyi Lingka in Lhasa.

Krystyna Cech

Harry William Gilbert Staunton 1908–1945

Harry Staunton was born on 19 May 1908 in Redhill, near Durban, South Africa where his father, Gilbert Patrick Staunton, practised as a doctor. At around the age of ten he left South Africa and became a pupil at Norwich Grammar School. On finishing school in 1925, he registered as a medical student at St. Bartholomew's Hospital, London where he graduated in 1931. He began his military training at Aldershot the same year. In 1934, he joined the Indian Medical Service and left for Bombay on the HMS Dorsetshire. His first posting was as Lieutenant on probation in Rawalpindi where he took charge of the Indian Medical Hospital. He helped with the rescue work at Quetta after the earthquake in 1934, and was promoted to the rank of Captain in February 1935. Thereafter, he was with Western Command, Quetta where he was practising as a specialist in Otology, Rhinology and Laryngology. On 7 January 1940, he was appointed Captain on deputation with the Lhasa Mission and from August 1940 to January 1942, he was Civil Surgeon Bhutan and Tibet. In 1942, he met his future wife, Silvia, a nurse in the Queen Alexandra's Indian Medical Nursing Service in Bombay. At the time of his death in 1945, he was Registrar of a large general hospital in Bombay. Major Staunton died in an aircrash on 22 November 1945 when returning to India from England where he had been on compassionate leave to visit his mother. The plane crashed shortly after take-off from Yeovilton, Somerset, killing

Harry Staunton
Unknown Photographer,
c. 1940–1942
PRM 1999.23.2.5.

all 27 passengers and crew. His widow gave birth to their second child, a daughter, a week later in Bombay.

Harry Staunton was one of two Westerners ever to have witnessed the Installation ceremony of a Dalai Lama (that of the current 14th Dalai Lama, Tenzin Gyatso). He was present on the second day (23 February 1940) of the eight-day ceremony with Basil Gould and some fifty members of the Mission staff (Croston 2000). When Basil Gould returned to Gangtok, Staunton stayed on in Lhasa with the task of planning and supervising the building of a new Mission hospital which was completed in August 1940. He treated many Lhasa residents as well as villagers and nomads who travelled from far afield for medical treatment. He reputedly treated the young Dalai Lama for measles in 1942. Unfortunately none of Staunton's diaries or reports have survived, and we have no written documentation of his time in Lhasa. However, it can be assumed that the medical conditions he treated would not have been too dissimilar to those listed in a report by William Morgan, the doctor for the 1936 Mission – venereal disease being the most common ailment. Staunton was assisted in his duties by Dr Rai Sahib Tonyot, a Sikkimese doctor.

Staunton's black and white photographs and colour film reveal a natural curiosity in his physical and social surroundings. His album traces the journey he made with Mission members from Gangtok to Lhasa in twenty-two stages. The team travelled in the dead of winter in order to reach Lhasa in time for the Dalai Lama's Installation ceremony. Some of the ceremonies recorded by Staunton at this time would not have been exclusive to the Installation, but rather those celebrated every year at the time of the Tibetan New Year (Losar). His photographs of what he calls 'Devil Dancing' are part of an exorcism ritual (*gutor*) which is performed in every Tibetan monastic community at the end of the year. There are also photographs of social occasions shared with members of the Tibetan aristocracy, including adults and children.

It is clear that Staunton felt comfortable using his camera as he walked the streets of Lhasa, suggesting his acceptance by the Tibetan people. This must have been due in large part to his role as Mission doctor and his success in treating the various illnesses of the local population (without charge). Staunton's achievements had a knock-on effect for the rest of the Mission as Hugh Richardson wrote: 'Over the years our friends among lamas and monks as well as laymen continued to widen, helped greatly by the work of doctors at the Hospital of the British Mission at Dekyi Lingka.' (Richardson 1993:8)

Staunton Collection

The Staunton collection at the Pitt Rivers Museum was donated by his daughter Diana Hughes in 1999. It comprises a personal album of 341 black and white photographs (Tibet 154, Bhutan 25, Sikkim 19, India 51, South Africa 87, family photographs 5) of various sizes, but mostly 120mm x 90mm. There are also 80 loose prints of Tibet, Bhutan and

Sikkim and 68 of India (some of which duplicate those in the album). In addition, there are four spools of 8mm colour film (now transferred to video and DVD) shot in Bhutan and Tibet.

The photographs of Tibet include Tibetan nobility (Tsarong, Taring, Doring, members of the Kashag), monk officials (the Dalai Lama and his family, the Regent, Kala Lama, the Nechung Oracle, Mission members (Gould, Richardson, Staunton, Norbhu) and friends (Fox, Betty Hughes, Humphries, Thornburgh) and General Wu of the Chinese Mission. There are photographs of topographical interest taken en route between Gangtok and Lhasa (Natu La, Yatung, Phari, Chusul, Chaksam) and of anthropological interest (travellers, pilgrims, villagers and nomads). Then there are scenes in and around Lhasa (featuring ceremonies at the Potala Palace, processions near the Jo khang temple, views of Drepung monastery, the houses of the Tsarong and Doring families, street scenes in Lhasa, masked dancers, Khampa dancers, the construction of the British Mission hospital in Lhasa and some of the patients, ferries and coracles, parties and picnics). Photographs of Sikkim include entertaining at the British Residency, Gangtok, the Sikkimese Royal family and a royal wedding. Photographs of Bhutan include the fortress-monastery of Paro, the Paro Penlop and his retinue and the treating of patients at Wangdu Phodang.

Film documentation includes a trip to Bhutan as well as the 1939–1940 Mission to Tibet. Film shot in Bhutan follows the lateral route from Gangtok into Bhutan as far as Paro via Ha. It features flowers (irises and primulas), fish (trout) and fishing, the Paro Penlop at Paro dzong and Staunton on horseback and bathing in a river. There are shots of organised games with Bhutanese children and punting on a lake with the Prime Minister, Raja Dorje.

Film shot in Tibet follows the route taken by the Mission to Lhasa with views of mountains (including Chomolhari) and villages, masked dances in the Eastern courtyard of the Potala palace on the end-of-year rituals (*gutor*), men dressed in ancient armour (for the *Trapchi Tsisher* ceremony), nobles, members of the Tsarong family dressed in fine silks in front of their Lhasa house and the Nechung Oracle in a trance. There is also film of the Potala with snow lying on the ground (a rare sight), the Western Gate, men gambling at *sho*, and the audience and dancers at the end-of-year masked dances in the Potala. Film shot in Gyantse shows the Kumbum, a market place with coral and carpet sellers, women selling *chang* (beer), a woman with a spindle, a girl knitting and women collecting water.

Krystyna Cech

I would like to acknowledge the kind help of Diana Hughes (née Staunton) in making all materials which she has collected about her father freely available to me. Also, Roger Croston was most helpful in pointing out sources.

Henry Martin and the Macdonald Collection

Henry Martin in Tibet
Unknown Photographer, *c.* 1911
PRM 1998.293.79 (detail).

The David Macdonald Collection at the Pitt Rivers Museum comprises 175 items – all photographic prints – showing people and places in southern Tibet, nearly all of which were taken by Henry Martin between 1908 and 1914. Images of Tibetan and Chinese officials, of the British trading posts at Gyantse and Yatung, of troops, monasteries and a variety of other scenes depict a way of life long since ended. Very little is known about the photographer, however, perhaps reflecting the fact that photography was neither his main employment nor a major source of income. In fact, Sergeant Henry Martin was a former labourer from London who served in Tibet with Younghusband, and who remained in Gyantse as a telegraphist, and later Head Clerk of the British Trade Agency there, from 1904 until he retired in 1931. This made him one of the two longest-serving Englishmen in Tibet and he was apparently twice married to Tibetan women, having two daughters (Alice and Maude) and a son (name unknown) (McKay 1997:98, 203; Ashencaen & Leonov 1995:102). In 1925, Martin was made a Member of the British Empire. (London Gazzette 1925, part 2):3779; Macdonald 1929:8) He died in 1931 not long after retiring, having found that despite 'his record of long faithful service ... hard to beat in the annals of a Government office', the British government was unwilling to correct an anomaly which reduced his pension by a third. (McKay 1997:203)

Martin was well regarded by his superiors, and early in his career he was given the task of photographing Tibetan notables for the Foreign Office in London. Provided with an 'official' camera for the purpose, he quickly learned to develop and print his own films (McKay 1997:99; Ashencaen & Leonov 1995:102). Unfortunately the Macdonald Collection includes no related documentation, but with the exception of two items the photographs are almost certainly all by Henry Martin. His initials 'H.M.' are given in the bottom right-hand corner of many of the images, though this is not always the case and sometimes the letters are obscured by what remains of the prints' corner fixings. These fixing marks reveal that before the photographs were donated to the Pitt Rivers Museum, they had been removed from one or more albums. The photographs themselves are contemporary gelatin silver prints (of typical size 14.0 × 8.5 cm), and most have been annotated on the back in pencil, possibly by Martin himself. Those prints which are dated include no year earlier than 1908 nor any later than 1914, suggesting that the pictures were probably all taken in the decade after the Younghusband Expedition, when British interest in Tibet remained high.

Gyantse features as the central location for nearly half the items in this collection, since this was where the photographer lived and worked. The telegraph sergeant photographed the old British fort there and recorded the movements of Chinese and Tibetan troops in the area. The hilltop fortress (*dzong*) at Gyantse is also portrayed and is visible in a series of fourteen prints showing Tibetan sporting events held on a plain outside the city. A particular focus of the collection, though, is trade, and reflecting this are images of the British Trade Agencies in Gyantse and, more especially, Yatung. Much official business passed through the British residency at Yatung, and pictured here are many of the diplomatic and administrative personnel who visited the trading post, with portraits of Lönchen Shatra, the Prime Minister of Tibet; Miru Gyalwa, described as a 'Tibetan Trade Agent'; and even one image of the 13th Dalai Lama, sheltering there on his flight from Lhasa to Darjeeling in 1910. Daily life at the residency is hinted at in views of the tennis court and a party of players which includes David Macdonald. More than a dozen other photographs of Macdonald, the Trade Agent at Gangtok, suggest that he and Martin had regular contact with each other, and it was probably through Macdonald, who was half-Sikkimese and an important figure in the region, that Martin gained access to many of his subjects. MacDonald, in his memoirs, however, makes no mention of the photographer, but this is consistent with the view that because Martin was of low standing, and not a high-ranking or diplomatic figure, little evidence of his life was ever committed to paper (McKay 1997: 203). The images are thus all that remain, and a number of these were reproduced in publications by both David Macdonald and also Sir Charles Bell. Later Henry Martin's son sold part of his father's archive to Macdonald, whose name it assumed when his daughter donated the collection to the Pitt Rivers Museum in 1995.

Among the other items in the collection are both exterior and interior views of various monasteries, including those at Gyantse, Kundeling, Naining, Phari, Sera, Shari, Tsechen, and one near Chumbi. In a courtyard of the monastery at Tenjoling, masked lamas are pictured performing a ritual dance, while another series of prints shows the ceremonial pageant surrounding the Chinese escort of the Panchen Lama, *circa* 1911. Other images show upper-class Tibetan women (recognised as such, a note says, by their 'long sleeves'); clerks and their orderlies; a magistrate in his robes; and a Chinese official with his bodyguard; and there are pictures, too, of minstrels, a beggar woman, a tinker, various indigenous animals, and also several landscapes, notably one of a frozen waterfall at Dota in the Chumbi valley. Glass plate copy negatives for eleven of these prints survive in the Bell Collection at the PRM, as do negatives for other photographs by Martin. While his work may not always be of the highest artistic quality, Henry Martin's photographic legacy nonetheless provides a valuable record of life in Tibet during the early part of the last century, particularly, in this collection, his images of political, military and local bureaucratic figures of the time, as well, of course, as those of certain monasteries and other buildings more recently destroyed.

Philip N. Grover

Bibliography

Anderson, Benedict, *Imagined Communities: Reflections on the Origin and Spread of Nationalism*, Verso, London, 1983–1991 edition.

Appadurai, Arjun (ed.), *The Social Life of Things: Commodities in Cultural Perspective*, Cambridge University Press, Cambridge, 1986.

Ashencaen, Deborah and Leonov, Gennady, *The Mirror of Mind: Art of Vajrayana Buddhism*, sale catalogue, Spink and Son, London, June 1995.

Bann, S. Stephen, *The Clothing of Clio: A Study of the Representation of History in Nineteenth-Century Britain and France*, Cambridge University Press, Cambridge, 1984.

Barker, Ralph, *One Man's Jungle: a biography of F. Spencer Chapman.* Chatto & Windus, London, 1975.

——— *Image, Music, Text*, Stephen Heath trans., Fontana, London, 1977.

Barthes, Roland, *Camera Lucida*, Richard Howard trans., Fontana, London, 1986.

Bell, Charles, *Portrait of a Dalai Lama: The Life and Times of the Great Thirteenth*, Wisdom Publications, London, 1987 [1946].

——— *Manual of Colloquial Tibetan*, Baptist Mission Press, Calcutta, 1905.

——— *The People of Tibet*, Clarendon Press, Oxford, 1928.

——— *The Religion of Tibet*, Clarendon Press, Oxford, 1931.

——— *Tibet: Past and Present*, Clarendon Press, Oxford, 1924.

——— 'A Year in Lhasa', *Geographical Journal*, vol. 63, 1924, pp. 89–105.

Berger, John, 'The Uses of Photography', *About Looking*, Writers and Readers Cooperative, London, 1980.

Billington, J., 'Captain H W G Staunton (I.M.S), Lhasa 1940', *The Tibet Society Journal*, 198?, pp. 10–12.

Bishop, Peter, *The Myth of Shangri-La: Tibet, Travel Writing and the Western Creation of Sacred Landscape*, Athlone Press, London, 1989.

——— 'The Potala and Western Place Making', *The Tibet Journal*, Library of Tibetan Works & Archives, Dharamsala, vol. XIX, No. 2, 1994.

Bishop, Peter, 'Glimpsing Tibet: A Landscape of Closure and Loss', *Literature and Travel*, vol. 6(2), 1997, pp. 56–72.

Brauen , Martin, *Traumwelt Tibet: Westliche Trugbilder*, Haupt, Bern, 2000.

Candler, Edmund, *The Unveiling of Lhasa*, Edward Arnold & co., London, 1905.

Clifford, James, 'Travelling Cultures', *Routes: Travel and Translation in the late Twentieth Century*, Harvard University Press, Cambridge, Mass. and London, 1997.

Croston, Roger, 'Sixty Years Since The Return to the Throne', *The Journal of The Tibet Society and Tibet Relief Fund of the United Kingdom*, 2000, pp. 10–11.

——— 'The Story of AC4YN – A Radio Adventure in Tibet, 1936', *Radcom*, June 2002a, pp. 39–40.

Ringang in New Year Dress
(opposite)
Hugh Richardson, *c.* 1936–1945

Chang Ngopa Rinzin Dorje (known as Ringang; 1904–1945) wearing gyaluche *dress – the ceremonial dress worn at New Year and believed to have been worn by the Yarlung dynasty rulers of Tibet (7th–9th centuries AD). Ringang was Translator to the Kashag (Tibetan Cabinet) and the Magistrate of Purang, a district in southern Tibet. By 1936, he was an offical of the 6th rank, which meant he could normally only wear silk in his own home and was not entitled to wear the amulet box which higher officials wore on their heads. In 1913, he had been one of the Tibetan boys sent (by Charles Bell and the 13th Dalai Lama) to be educated at Rugby school in England. On his return, he was responsible for installing electricity in Lhasa. At the time of the 14th Dalai Lama's Installation in 1940, Ringang was a civil officer in charge of organising and commanding the 600-strong cavalry that attended the event. Basil Gould noted: 'As District Magistrate of a distant part of Tibet (where his wife sometimes discharged his duties), engineer of the mint and of the hydro-electric installation and interpreter to the Cabinet, he had his hands full.' (1957)*
PRM 2001.59.18.15.1.

——— 'Lieutenant Colonel Sir Evan Yorke Nepean, Baronet', draft copy of an article for the *Journal of the Royal Signals*, 2002b.

Dalai Lama, *Freedom in Exile, The Autobiography of His Holiness the Dalai Lama of Tibet*, Hodder & Stoughton, London, 1990.

David-Néel, Alexandra, *Voyage d'une Parisienne à Lhassa (My journey to Lhasa; the personal story of the only white woman who succeeded in entering the forbidden city)*, Harper & Brothers, New York and London, 1927.

De Alarcón, Marina, 'Charles Bell', *Collectors: Collecting for the Pitt Rivers Museum*, Pitt Rivers Museum, Oxford, 1996.

Debrett's Peerage, *Debrett's People of Today*, 2002.

Desideri, Ippolito, *An Account of Tibet*, Ch'eng Wen Publishing Company, Taipei, 1971.

Dodin, Thierry and Räther, Hans, *Imagining Tibet: Perceptions, Projections and Fantasies*, Wisdom Publications, Boston, 2001.

Douglas, Ed, 'Hugh Richardson Obituary', *The Guardian*, London, 5 January 2001.

Edwards, Elizabeth, 'Photographs as Objects of Memory', in Kwint, Marius, Breward, Christopher and Aynsley, Jeremy eds, *Material memories: Design and Evocation*, Berg, Oxford, 1999.

——— *Raw Histories: Photographs, Anthropology and Museums*, Berg, Oxford, 2001a.

——— 'Photography and the 'performance of History', *Kronos: Journal of Cape History*, no. 27, 2001b, pp. 15–29.

——— 'Material Beings; objecthood and ethnographic photographs', *Visual Studies*, no. 17(1), 2002, pp. 67–75.

French, Patrick, *Younghusband: The Last Great Imperial Adventurer*, HarperCollins, London, 1994.

Gao, Delphine, 'The Eye of the Living Buddha, the First Photographer of Tibet', *Photographer International*, no. 39, Taipei, 1998.

Gell, Alfred, *Art and Agency: An Anthropological theory*, Clarendon Press, Oxford, 1998.

Giorgi, Agostino Antonio, *Alphabetum Tibetanum missionum apostolicarum commodo editum Romae*, 1762.

Goldstein, Melvyn, *Anthropological Study of the Tibetan Political System*, Ph.D. dissertation, University of Washington, 1968.

——— 'Lhasa Street Songs: Political and Social Satire in Traditional Tibet', *The Tibet Journal*, Library of Tibetan Works & Archives, Dharamsals, no. 7 (1 and 2), 1982, pp. 56–57.

——— *A History of Modern Tibet, 1913–1951: The Demise of the Lamaist State*, University of California Press, Berkeley, 1989.

Gombrich, Ernst, *Art and Illusion*, Princeton University Press, Princeton, 2000.

Gould, Basil, 'Report on the discovery, Recognition and Installation of the Fourteenth Dalai Lama', Government of India Press, New Delhi, 1941.

——— *The Jewel in the Lotus: Recollections of an Indian Political Officer*, Chatto & Windus, London, 1957.

'Gould, Basil', entry in *The Dictionary of National Biography*, Oxford University Press, Oxford, 1995.

Hallisey, Charles, 'Roads Taken and Not Taken in the Study of Theravada Buddhism', in Lopez, Donald ed., *Curators of the Buddha: The Study of Buddhism under Colonialism*, University of Chicago Press, Chicago, 1995.

Hansen, Peter, 'Tibetan Horizon: Tibet and the Cinema in the Early Twentieth Century', in Dodin, Thierry and Rather, Heinz. eds, *Imagining Tibet: Perceptions, Projections and Fantasies*, Wisdom Publications, Boston, 2001.

——— 'The Dancing Lamas of Everest: Cinema, Orientalism and Anglo–Tibetan Relations in the 1920s', *The American Historical Review*, vol. 101, Issue 3, 1996, pp. 712–747.

Harris, Clare, *In the Image of Tibet: Tibetan Painting after 1959*, Reaktion, London, 1999.

——— *A Camera in Tibet: Photographs of Charles Bell and Spencer Chapman*, Atlas Ltd Editions, London, 2000. (catalogue to exhibition held in the Atlas Galley, London, 2000)

——— 'The Politics and Personhood of Tibetan Buddhist Icons', in Thomas, Nicholas and Pinney, Christopher eds, *Beyond Aesthetics: Art and the technologies of enchantment*, Berg, London, 2001.

Hilton, James, *Lost Horizon*, Macmillan, London, 1933.

Hoskins, Janet, *Biographical Objects: how things tell the stories of people's lives*, Routledge, New York and London, 1998.

Hughes, Diana, 'Report on a visit to Tibet', *Tibet Alive*, forthcoming.

Khe smad, bsod names, *Rgas po'i lo rgyus 'bel gtam*, LTWA, Dharamsala, 1982.

Kipling, Rudyard, *Kim*, London, 1905 [1987 edition, Harmondsworth Penguin].

Kuhn, Annette, *Family Secrets: acts of memory and imagination*, Verso, London, 1995.

Lamb, Alastair, *British India and Tibet 1766–1910*, Routledge & Kegan Paul, London, 1986.

——— *Tibet, China and India 1914–1950. A History of Imperial Diplomacy*, Roxford Books, Hertsfordshire, 1989.

Landon, Perceval, *Lhasa*, London, 1905.

Langford, Martha, *Suspended Conversations: the afterlife of memory in photographic albums*, McGill-Queens University Press, Montreal and London, 2001.

Lopez, Donald, *Prisoners of Shangri-la: Tibetan Buddhism and the West*, University of Chicago Press, Chicago and London, 1998.

——— *Curators of the Buddha: The Study of Buddhism under Colonialism*, University of Chicago Press, Chicago, 1995.

Macdonald, David, *The Land of the Lama: A Description of a Country of Contrast, and of its Cheerful, Happy-go-lucky People of Hardy Nature and Curious Customs; Their Religion, Ways of Living, Trade and Social Life*, Seeley, Service & Co., Limited, London, 1929.

——— *Twenty Years in Tibet: Intimate and Personal Experiences of the Closed Land among all Classes of its People from the Highest to the Lowest*, Seeley, Service & Co., Limited, London, 1932.

Mackenzie, Maureen Anne, *Androgynous Objects: String Bags and Gender in Central New Guinea*, Harwood Academic Publishers, Chur, Switzerland and Philadelphia, 1991.

McGovern, William Montgomery, *To Lhasa in disguise, a secret expedition through mysterious Tibet*, Century Co, New York and London, 1924.

McKay, Alex, '"Truth", Perception and Politics: The British Construction of an Image of Tibet', in Dodin, Thierry and Rather, Heinz eds, *Imagining Tibet: Perceptions, Projections, and Fantasies*, Wisdom Publications, Boston, 2001.

——— *Tibet and the British Raj: The Frontier Cadre 1904 – 1947*, Curzon, Richmond, 1997.

——— 'The Other Great Game: Politics and Sport in Tibet 1904– 1947', in *The International Journal of the History of Sport*, no. 11.3, 1994.

Mission Diaries 1936–1937, Related Documents Collection Pitt Rivers Museum.

Nepean, Evan, 'The Story of AC4YN, the first amateur radio station on the Roof of the World', manuscript in the Pitt Rivers Museum, n.d.

——— 'The AC4YN Story – a Tibetan Adventure circa 1936–1937', *73 Magazine*, 1982, pp. 10–12.
'Evan Nepean', obituary in *The Times*, London, Saturday, 6 April, 2002.
Nordstrom, Alison Devine. 'Photography of Samoa: production, dissemination, and use' in Blanton, Casey (ed.) *Picturing Paradise: Colonial Photography of Samoa, 1875 to 1925 Daytona Beach Southeast Museum of Photography.* Daytona Beach Community College, 1995.
O'Connor, Frederick, *The Geographical Magazine*, vol. VI, no 2, London, 1937.
Pemba, Tsewang, *Young Days in Tibet*, Jonathan Cape, London, 1957.
Petech, Luciano, *Aristocracy and Government in Tibet, 1728–1959*, Instituto Italiano per il Medio ed Estremo Oriente, Roma, 1973.
Photographers International (journal) Special Issue, *The First Photographer of Tibet: Lopsang Jampal Loodjor Tenzin Gyatso Demo*, no. 39, August 1998, Taipei Photographers International.
Poole, Deborah, *Vision, Race and Modernity: A Visual Economy of the Andean Image World*, Princeton University Press, Princeton, 1997.
Porto, Nuno, 'Picturing the Museum: photography and the work of mediation in the Third Portuguese Empire', in Bouquet, Mary ed., *Academic Anthropology and the Museum*, Berghahn, Oxford, 2001.
Rabinowitz, Paula, *They Must be Represented: The politics of documentary*, Verso, London, 1994.
Richards, Thomas, *The Imperial Archive: Knowledge and the Fantasy of Empire*, Verso, London, 1993.
Richardson, Hugh, *Ceremonies of the Lhasa Year*, Michael Aris ed., Serindia, London, 1993.
——— *High Peaks, Pure Earth: Collected Writings on Tibetan History and Culture*, Michael Aris (ed.), Serindia, London, 1998.
Ryan, James, *Picturing Empire: Photography and the Visualization of the British Empire*, Reaktion Books, London, 1997.
Sassoon, Joanna, 'Photographic Materiality in the Age of Digital Reproduction' in Edwards, Elizabeth and Hart, J. eds, *Photographs. Objects, Histories*, Routledge, London, forthcoming.
Schwartz, Joan M., '"We Make our Tools and our Tools make us": Lessons from Photographs for the Practice, Politics and Poetics of Diplomatics', *Archivaria*, no. 50, 1995, pp. 40–75.
Shelton, Albert, *Pioneering in Tibet*, Fleming H Revel Company, New York, 1925.
Spencer Chapman, Frederick, *Northern Lights*, Chatto & Windus, London, 1932.
——— *Watkins' Last Expedition*, Chatto & Windus, London, 1934.
——— 'Tibetan Horizon', *Sight and Sound*, London, vol. 6, 1937, pp. 122–125.
——— *Lhasa the Holy City*, Chatto & Windus, London, 1938.
——— 'A Kodachrome Film of Tibet', *The Photographic Journal*, London, vol. 78, April 1938, pp. 262–266.
——— *Helvellyn to Himalaya*, Chatto & Windus, London, 1940.
——— *Memoirs of a Mountaineer* (combined reprint of *Lhasa: The Holy City* and *Helvellyn to Himalaya*),The Reprint Society and Chatto & Windus, London, 1945.
——— *The Jungle is Neutral*, Chatto & Windus, London, 1948.
——— *Living Dangerously*, Chatto & Windus, London, 1953.
——— *Lightest Africa*, Chatto & Windus, London, 1955.
'Frederick Spencer Chapman', obituary in *The Times*, 10 August 1971.
Tagg, John, *The Burden of Representation: Essays on Photographies and Histories*, Macmillan Education, Basingstoke, 1988.

——— 'The Pencil of History', in Petro, Patrice ed., *Fugitive Images: From Photography to Video*, Indiana University Press, Bloomington, 1995.

Tailing, Wangdor, *bkras zur tshang gyi gsang ba'i gtam rgyud*, Tibetan People's Publishing House, Lhasa, 1997.

Taring, Rinchen Dolma (Mary), *Daughter of Tibet*, Murray, London, 1970.

Thomas, Nicholas, *Entangled Objects: Exchange, Material Culture, and Colonialism in the Pacific*, Harvard University Press, Cambridge, Mass. and London, 1991.

Tsarong, Dundul Namgyal, *In the Service of His Country*, Snow Lion Publications, Ithaca, New York, 2000.

——— *What Tibet Was, As seen by a native photographer*, New Delhi, 1990.

Tsering, Deki, *Dalai Lama, My Son. A Mother's Story*, Virgin, London, 2000.

Turner, Samuel, *An Account of an Embassy to the Court of the Teshoo Lama, in Tibet*, London, 1806.

Van Alphen, Ernst, *Caught by History: Holocaust effects in contemporary art, literature and theory*, Stanford University Press, Stanford, 1997.

Waddell, Laurence Austine, *The Buddhism of Tibet: or Lamaism*, W. Heffer, Cambridge, 1971 [1894].

——— *Among the Himalayas*, Westminster, London, 1899.

——— *Lhasa and its Mysteries with a Record of the Expedition of 1903–4*, London, 1905.

Wangdu, Sonam, *The Discovery of the 14th Dalai Lama*, Klett Thai Publications, Bangkok, 1975.

Who's Who in Tibet, Government of India Press. Calcutta, 1938 (L/P&S/12/418517. India Office, Library)

Who was Who, 1996–2000: a companion to Who's Who containing the biographies of those who died during the period 1996–2000, A & C Black, London, October 2001.

Younghusband, Francis, *India and Tibet*, Oxford University Press, Hong Kong, 1985.

Yuthok, Dorje Yudon, *House of Turquoise Roof*, Snow Lion Publications, Ithaca, New York, 1990.

Three Men at New Year (next page)
Frederick Spencer Chapman, 1937

Three lay officials dressed for Tibetan New Year ceremonies in the gyaluche *costume – robes and ornaments of the Yarlung dynasty rulers of Tibet (7th–9th centuries AD). The huge amber, turquoise and gold breast plates, known as* ringyen *(ancient precious ornaments), were only removed from the Potala treasury on this occasion and for certain events involving the Dalai Lama (such as his entrance as a student into Drepung monastery). The man on the right (with red hat) is Kyibu, who had been one of the four boys sent by the 13th Dalai Lama to study at Rugby school in England in 1913.*
PRM 1998.157.75.

Index